# UNDERSTANDING
# MENTAL RETARDATION

# UNDERSTANDING
# MENTAL RETARDATION

*A Guide for Social Workers*

By

## DALE BRANTLEY, M.S.S.W.

*Director, Division of Social Services*
*Chauncey Sparks Center for Developmental*
*and Learning Disorders*
*University of Alabama at Birmingham*

**C H A R L E S  C  T H O M A S • P U B L I S H E R**
*Springfield • Illinois • U. S. A.*

*Published and Distributed Throughout the World by*
CHARLES C THOMAS • PUBLISHER
2600 South First Street
Springfield, Illinois 62794-9265

© *1988 by* CHARLES C THOMAS • PUBLISHER

ISBN 0-398-05413-4

Library of Congress Catalog Card Number: 87-18094

*Printed in the United States of America*
*Q-R-3*

*Library of Congress Cataloging in Publication Data*

Brantley, Dale.
    Understanding mental retardation.

    Bibliography: p.
    Includes index.
    1. Mental retardation. 2. Social workers. I. Title.
[DNLM: 1. Mental Retardation. 2. Social Work.
WM 300 B92lu]
RC570.B73   1988        616.85'88        87-18094
ISBN 0-398-05413-4

*For Patricia, Phillip and Amy*

# CONTRIBUTORS

**Harriet H. Cloud M.S., R.D.**

*Director, Division of Nutrition*
*Chauncey Sparks Center for Developmental & Learning Disorders*
*University of Alabama at Birmingham*

**Ernest E. Singletary, Ed.D.**

*Associate Professor*
*Department of Special Education*
*University of Alabama at Birmingham*

**Michael D. Wesson, O.D., M.S.**

*Director, Division of Vision Function*
*Chauncey Sparks Center for Developmental & Learning Disorders*
*University of Alabama at Birmingham*

# FOREWORD

SOCIAL WORKERS who work with mentally retarded/developmentally disabled persons and their families face a challenge of combining psychosocial and systems expertise with complex and ever-changing biophysiological information. Through use of the information provided in this book regarding the causes and consequences of mental retardation, the social worker's capacity to fulfill this challenge is greatly enhanced.

The book contains a discussion of 23 selected syndromes which cover the range of etiologies and manifestations of mental retardation. This should provide the reader with basic information about the syndromes described and also provide a framework for seeking knowledge and understanding about other causes and consequences of mental retardation.

The legal provisions of services in the United States for persons with mental retardation/developmental disabilities are clearly outlined in Chapter Three. Included are those of the Administration on Developmental Disabilities, Children's Bureau, Social Security Administration, and Departments of Education and Rehabilitation Services. The definition of terms included with the legislative base of services provides an excellent foundation for gaining a beginning understanding of the myriad of services for mentally retarded/developmentally disabled persons and the complexity of their service system.

For the student or practitioner unfamiliar with the field of mental retardation/developmental disabilities, the case examples used in the text provide rich illustration of the range of manifestations of genetic conditions with attention given to the treatment concerns as well as identification of etiology. Emphasis is maintained upon the role of social work and the ways in which the social worker is able to make a contribution to the services and care provided to the child and family.

It is often difficult for social workers to envision their role in an interdisciplinary setting. This is especially true when the problems faced by the clients are complex, require multiple medical specialists to diagnose and prescribe treatment and are chronic. The role of the social work practitioner in mental retardation/developmental disabilities has been greatly enhanced through the training, service and research activities of the more than 40 University Affiliated Facilities across the United States. These facilities have developed exemplary interdisciplinary training over the past 20 years for students preparing to work in the field of mental retardation/developmental disabilities. The author has utilized many examples from his practice in a University Affiliated Facility which illustrates many ways in which the social worker can make a significant contribution with these clients and their families. This book not only provides clearly written content in mental retardation/developmental disabilities but also demonstrates the many facets of social work involvement which have developed.

MARGARET A. WEST, M.S.W., PH.D.

*Director Social Work*
*Child Development and Mental Retardation Center*
*Assistant Research Professor*
*Special Education*
*University of Washington*
*Seattle, Washington*

# INTRODUCTION

THIS BOOK is written as a teaching guide for social work students and practitioners interested in the field of mental retardation. The author's intent is to provide fundamental information about mental retardation, its causes and consequences, and particularly its impact on the family.

Social workers in the field of mental retardation always have been concerned with the stress that mental retardation brings to the family. This is a proper concern for social work, but the author believes strongly that social workers need more than traditional social work skills to work successfully in the field of mental retardation. In order to collaborate with families and with other professionals on issues related to mental retardation, social workers additionally need broader knowledge about the physical, mental, health, and etiological aspects of mental retardation.

A combination of technical knowledge and traditional social work skills, then, appears essential for successful intervention in this field. Consequently, the author's primary goal in this book is to introduce social work students and practitioners to the multiple facets of mental retardation. It is not an in-depth work on the subject, nor is it an attempt to cover all the issues related to mental retardation. The book has fundamental reference value and should serve as a stimulus for readers to seek additional knowledge in all areas of handicapping conditions.

The book provides a general description of mental retardation, including definitions, causes, prevention strategies, and implications for social work research. The roles of the major disciplines in the field of mental retardation are defined to illustrate the significance of comprehensive interdisciplinary care for individuals who are mentally retarded. People who are handicapped have rights guaranteed by federal legislation which insure due process and equal protection in receiving services. Therefore, the book also presents an overview of legal provisions pertaining to the area of mental retardation/developmental disabilities.

To illustrate the multiple problems associated with mental retardation, the author discusses 23 selected syndromes. Some of these syndromes admittedly are rarely seen. However, the selected syndromes are chosen because they (1) represent different etiologies, (2) manifest various signs and symptoms, and (3) demonstrate a wide range of handicaps, in both type and severity. The goal of the author is to emphasize that syndromes involving mental retardation — whether they are seen frequently or infrequently — possess certain mental, physical, and neurological characteristics that aid the diagnostic process and directly affect the treatment plan. Some characteristics are common to all syndromes, while other features are unique to particular disorders.

In this work mental retardation is described as a complex set of psychosocial — biophysical factors, a combination which often has a devastating effect on family life. In such instances, persons with mental retardation require a diversity of services. As the case histories contained in this work demonstrate, social work plays a major role in providing these services.

Significant progress has been made in the field of mental retardation, but much remains to be done. Perhaps the major task facing social workers, and all professionals concerned with mental retardation, is to perpetuate the concept of prevention, a concept introduced in the early sixties. In the past, social work has responded to many challenges. The present challenge in the field of mental retardation is consistent with the basic philosophy of social work: to promote a more positive life-style for our fellow human beings who comprise this segment of society.

D.B.

# ACKNOWLEDGMENTS

I AM INDEBTED to many people for their assistance in writing this book. First, I would like to acknowledge the encouragement and helpful suggestions given to me by Gary Myers, M.D., Director of the Chauncey Sparks Center for Developmental and Learning Disorders, University of Alabama at Birmingham (UAB). Other colleagues at the Sparks Center to whom I am especially grateful for their review of the material for scientific accuracy include: Harriet H. Cloud, M.S., R.D.; John B. Thornton, D.M.D.; Michael D. Wesson, O.D., M.S.; Shirley Steele, R.N., C., Ph.D.; Carol Goossens, Ph.D.; and Lois Hayes, Ed.S.

Other helpful ideas were contributed by several staff members of UAB's Laboratory of Medical Genetics. These include: Jerry N. Thompson, Ph.D., and Paula R. Scarbrough, M.D. Also, I am indebted to Ernest Singletary, Ed.D., Associate Professor, Department of Special Education, University of Alabama at Birmingham, for writing Chapter Three.

Finally, I extend my sincere appreciation to Katherine Howard, M.A. for her assistance in editing the material. Additionally, I am most grateful for the efforts of Roni Crocker, Sheila Foltz, and Catherine Terry, staff members at the Sparks Center, who typed the manuscript.

# CONTENTS

# UNDERSTANDING
# MENTAL RETARDATION

# Part I

CHAPTER 1 provides a general description of mental retardation including definitions, causes, prevention strategies, and implications for social work research. To illustrate the importance of comprehensive, interdisciplinary care for individuals who are mentally retarded, Chapter 2 presents a summary description of the major disciplines in the field of mental retardation. Excluded are disciplines that provide educational and vocational habilitation services. In recent years much progress has been made through Federal legislation to insure that people who are handicapped have equal rights and protection in receiving services. Chapter 3 covers the legal provisions of services in the United States for persons with mental retardation/developmental disabilities.

# Chapter One

# MENTAL RETARDATION: AN OVERVIEW

## INTRODUCTION

MENTAL RETARDATION is of major importance to many disciplines including social work. However, knowing that mental retardation produces an inherently stressful impact and that it requires, in many cases, lifelong support from a variety of clinical and educational specialties is fundamental to understanding the role of social work in the field of mental retardation. Traditionally, social work has been concerned primarily with the impact that mental disorders have on the lives of people in terms of personal and family distress. This is a valid concern, but successful social work intervention in the field of mental retardation must go beyond the more traditional skills long used by social work. It must include a broader knowledge base concerning mental retardation, its causes, and its consequences.[1]

## DEFINITIONS AND DESCRIPTIONS

Depending on the systems of classification, estimates indicate that from 1 to 3 percent of the population in the United States are mentally retarded, although, because of the difficulty of classification, an exact figure is unknown. Many times, people with mental retardation do not fit neatly into any one classification; in fact, wide variations as to the type and degree of handicaps are found from person to person. Some are profoundly mentally retarded with several associated handicaps and require lifelong protective care; others are only mildly affected and achieve and maintain productive, independent lives.

The definition of mental retardation, as formulated by the American Association on Mental Deficiency, is a widely used system of classification and is generally accepted by health professionals throughout the world. According to this definition, an individual is considered mentally retarded if the person in question has "significant sub-average general intellectual functioning resulting in or associated with concurrent impairments in adaptive behavior and manifested during the developmental period" (Grossman, 1983, p. 11). The first part of the definition refers to "sub-average intelligence" or an IQ level of 70 or below, obtained on an individually administered standardized test designed to measure intellectual functioning. In addition to intellectual limitations, there must be evidence of delays, defects or deficits in acquiring "personal independence and social responsibility expected for age and cultural group as determined by clinical assessment and, usually, standardized scales" (Grossman, 1983, p. 11). The final part of the definition considers the age at which the mental retardation is manifested. To fall within the definition, mental retardation must be present during the developmental years, which is the time between conception and 18 years of age. For example, a 2-year-old who suffered brain damage as the result of an accident would have a diagnosis of mental retardation; an 18-year-old who was brain damaged from the same accident would have a diagnosis of "brain damage."

Mental retardation is separated into four levels: mild, moderate, severe and profound. Table 1 shows the levels of retardation with corresponding IQ values.

TABLE 1

Levels of Retardation According to IQ Range
(American Association on Mental Deficiency)

| *Term* | *IQ Range for Level* |
|---|---|
| Mild Mental Retardation | 50–55 to 70 |
| Moderate Mental Retardation | 35–40 to 50–55 |
| Severe Mental Retardation | 20–25 to 35–40 |
| Profound Mental Retardation | Below 20 or 25 |
| Unspecified | |

IQ scores are obtained by using standardized tests for certain age groups. The Bayley Scales of Infant Development is an example of a test used to evaluate children who are from 1 month to 2½ years of age.

Since this test is dependent on non-verbal items, test results should be used with caution.

The Stanford Binet Intelligence Scale frequently is used to test children as well as adults. However, the Wechsler Intelligence Scale for Children — Revised (WISC-R) is preferred for older children, because it contains a number of subtests of language ability and performance and consequently allows the examiner to determine the child's strengths and weaknesses.

It is well to remember that intellectual development is influenced by many factors: heredity, culture, and environment, to name a few. Scores on IQ tests do not reflect motivation, creativity, mechanical ability and many other aspects of brain functioning, which may explain why some people who are otherwise mentally retarded perform adequately in their daily lives.

The great majority of the mentally retarded (probably between 75% to 85%) are mildly affected and are "educable." Many of these individuals appear to be normal with no physical or other manifestations of mental retardation. As young children, they may not reach certain developmental milestones on time, but mental retardation per se may not be suspected until the early school years when they fail to achieve academically at a normal pace. A two-year delay in academic performance can be expected, with grade achievement rarely surpassing the sixth-grade level. However, they have the potential to acquire independent living skills and to develop certain vocational skills. While many individuals who are mildly retarded show good social adjustment, some do not; personality or behavioral problems may limit their ability to adjust socially. Nevertheless, the majority remain in the open community working as semi-skilled or unskilled workers and in general maintain fairly normal lives without ever being identified as mentally retarded.

Individuals who are moderately retarded fit into what is called the "trainable" category and comprise about 10 percent of the mental retardation population (Chinn, Drew, & Logan, 1975). In addition to their intellectual limitations, they often have other handicaps including speech and language disorders, visual impairment, neurological problems, poor dental hygiene, poor dietary habits, and other health-related problems. With special help, they can acquire a limited number of basic competency and self-help skills. Some demonstrate limited potential for developing vocational and occupational skills and function satisfactorily under close supervision in a sheltered work situation.

The profoundly and severely retarded comprise about 3 percent of all mentally retarded individuals (Chinn et al., 1975). Many of them have little or no potential for independent living and require lifelong super-vised care. Frequently, they, too, are multi-handicapped with central nervous system abnormalities, musculoskeletal problems, sensory de-fects, and other health-related problems. Individuals who are severely and profoundly mentally retarded are likely to be diagnosed at birth or shortly thereafter because of apparent handicaps or stigmata that are present usually in conjunction with other types of pathology.

## ETIOLOGY

Mental retardation is not a phenomenon with a single cause; more than 200 causes have been identified. However, the etiological classifica-tion of mental retardation is complicated by the fact that the etiology is unknown in a large percentage of the cases; that percentage may be as high as 75 percent. Most tables of etiological classification of mental re-tardation show two major categories: genetic and acquired (Milunsky, 1975).

### Genetic Causes

Genetic disorders account for about 5 percent to 10 percent of all cases of mental retardation (Litch, 1978). Some geneticists report a higher percentage, but each year more disorders of mental retardation are being identified as having a genetic etiology. Among the genetic dis-orders of mental retardation, chromosomal abnormalities are the most common. One example is Down syndrome, which is a well-known and easily recognizable disorder. The fact that there is a preponderance of males who are mentally retarded (approximately 60% males to 40% fe-males) can be explained partially by genetic influences or what is called X-linked mental retardation. In fact, fragile X syndrome is thought to be the second most common chromosomal cause of mental retardation in males (Hagerman, McBogg & Hagerman, 1983). Most metabolic disorders such as phenylketonuria, galactosemia, homocystinuria, and maple syrup urine disease have a genetic etiology, but individually these disorders rarely are seen. Though the frequency of these disorders may seem small compared to other mental retardation syndromes, they nev-ertheless can be devastating and crippling when they do occur. Usually, genetic disorders come to the attention of health professionals early in the life of an affected child, either because they are identified at birth or because families suspect something is wrong and spontaneously seek diagnosis and treatment.

## Acquired Causes

Acquired causes of mental retardation involve non-heritable, environmental somatic factors that can occur *in utero,* perinatally or postnatally. As with genetic etiology, acquired causes of mental retardation can result in multiple and severe handicaps, but in the majority of the cases of mental retardation of this type, no identifiable physical characteristics are apparent. Furthermore, in contrast to cases involving more severe forms of mental retardation, most affected individuals in this category usually are not identified by their families; in fact, diagnosis is not likely until the early school years. If the diagnosis eventually is made, the cause well may be ascribed to psychosocial reasons. Without any clear-cut clinical evidence, the etiology is listed simply as unknown.

### Acquired Causes (Prenatal)

Infections, drugs, malformations, and prenatal injuries are just a few examples of early influences on embryonic development that can result in mental retardation along with physical and/or sensory anomalies. For example, several viruses and infectious organisms do more damage to the unborn child than they do to the mother. Cytomegalovirus (CMV) infections occurring during pregnancy can result in a number of birth defects in the child, including mental retardation. Another example of an infection occurring during pregnancy that can cause birth defects and mental retardation is toxoplasmosis, which is an intracellular parasite, not a virus. (The incidence of toxoplasmosis infections during pregnancy could be reduced if pregnant women did not handle cats or cat litter and avoided eating rare meats.) This type of infection occurring early in pregnancy can result in birth defects similar to the defects found in CMV. Other types of prenatal infections that can produce mental retardation are congenital syphilis, hepatitis, herpes simplex and congenital rubella, although rubella now is controllable because serologic testing and immunization are now available.

Drugs and toxic substances can result in complications during pregnancy, including bleeding, stillbirths and premature delivery. The deleterious effects of alcohol and smoking on the unborn fetus are now being brought to the attention of the public. Also, health professionals now are beginning to report that the use of cocaine during pregnancy has serious health consequences for the developing fetus and can leave the infant with permanent physical and mental damage.

Evidence is increasing that maternal malnutrition during pregnancy can cause mental retardation to the infant. An expectant mother who has thyroid deficiency or diabetes is at risk of having a mentally retarded child. Toxemia (high blood pressure, excessive weight gain and fluid retention) is most harmful to the infant in the later months of pregnancy, and if the condition is not promptly treated, brain damage can result. Of course, other hazards can prevent the mother from protecting and adequately nourishing the infant during pregnancy, but fortunately some disorders associated with mental retardation have been eliminated or almost eliminated through dietary management, antibiotics, vaccines, mass immunizations and other types of health intervention.

### Acquired Causes (Perinatal)

During the perinatal period the infant is vulnerable to birth injuries and other complications that can result in lifelong handicapping conditions. Asphyxia, or lack of oxygen at the time of birth, is considered to be a major cause of birth defects including mental retardation and cerebral palsy (Apgar & Beck, 1974). Any complication that cuts off the infant's supply of oxygen during the birth process increases the risk for brain damage.

Very small, premature babies with birthweights less than 2½ pounds are at risk for delayed development (Drillien, 1961; Parmelee & Haber, 1973). Women at risk for premature and low birthweight babies include teenage mothers, women more than 35 years of age, women with certain health problems, (diabetes, epilepsy), and women with histories of genetic diseases, as well as women who are poor, obese, and poorly nourished.

Pregnancy among teenagers has serious health consequences for both the mother and child. Young and physically immature mothers are at high risk for producing infants with developmental disabilities. These mothers have more obstetric problems than women in the "safe" childbearing range, and they tend to wait beyond the first trimester to seek prenatal care. They have high rates of toxemia, prolonged labor, premature delivery, and small-for-date infants. In general, they have a greater incidence of maternal complications and of fetal abnormalities, all of which are extremely high-risk factors for mental retardation (Haynes, 1980; Williams, 1982).

Many other perinatal problems are associated with mental retardation. They include placental anomalies, birth trauma, fetal malnutrition, post-maturity, hypoglycemia, hyperbilirubinemia, and multiple births (twins, triplets, etc.).

### Acquired Causes (Postnatal)

The early years of life represent a crucial time for the developing infant. Fortunately, most infants, after a successful gestation, are born free of complications and enter life as normal, healthy individuals. Nevertheless, certain conditions or influences can lead to serious and permanent disabilities, including mental retardation. Early childhood diseases, accidents, malnutrition, toxic substances, intracranial tumors, special sensory handicaps, asphyxia, environmental and social problems are frequently mentioned as mechanisms that can cause mental retardation during the postnatal period.

Social work is concerned primarily with the effects of the environment and the quality of life as causative factors in the child's development. The relationship between poverty and mental retardation has long been recognized, especially by the social work profession. In fact, socioeconomic conditions, according to many sources, may account for as much as 75 percent of all mental retardation. Malnutrition, unhealthy living conditions, poor child care, family emotional problems, and the inability to afford medical care comprise a few factors that contribute to the disproportionate frequency of mental retardation found among the poor. The impaired learning ability of some children frequently is blamed on "sensory deprivation" or the lack of stimuli in the home. Also, the effects of "inadequate" mothering and intellectually limited parents now are receiving attention as a risk factor in causing mental retardation (Kaminer & Cohen, 1983). However, further studies are needed to determine the prevalence of the problem. Data indicate that, whatever the reason, children born and raised in poverty are more likely to be diagnosed as mentally retarded than are children from middle- and upper-class backgrounds.

Child abuse and neglect are serious and pervasive problems, with more than one million cases being reported each year. Contrary to popular belief, the problem of child abuse is not confined to the poor but is found throughout the socioeconomic scale. One of the many negative effects of the maltreatment of children is the likelihood of mental retardation. Severe and prolonged malnutrition, for example, if present during the first year of life, may result in permanent damage to the brain and central nervous system (Scrimshaw, 1969). Additionally, the battered child with head injuries is likely to suffer severe and permanent brain damage. Whether pre-existing retardation is a causative agent for abuse is not clear because studies have shown that children who are different (i.e., the hyperactive, the handicapped and the mentally retarded) are at greater risk for abuse than the so-called "normal" child (Lieber, 1976). Evidence is mounting that abuse and neglect are causative agents in producing mental retardation (Crain & Millor, 1978; Runyan & Gould, 1985; Schilling, Schinke, Blythe & Barth, 1982).

Studies now are showing that children with AIDS have a wide variety of neurological and developmental abnormalities (Belman, et al., 1984). The causes of these abnormalities are thought to be related to prolonged hospitalizations, recurrent infections, and nutritional problems affecting the central nervous system.

There are several other causes of mental retardation during the postnatal period. These include: infections (e.g. encephalitis, meningitis), intoxications (e.g. lead poisoning), head trauma (e.g. accidents), special sensory handicaps (e.g. deafness or blindness), and asphyxia (e.g. near-drowning).

Much, however, still is not known about the causes of mental retardation. For the practicing social worker, a basic understanding of what is generally known about the etiology of mental retardation must be the first step in providing services and in helping to prevent the occurrence of such disorders.

## PREVENTION

Just as there is no simple explanation for the causes of mental retardation, no easy solution exists for its prevention. The question of whether or not mental retardation can be prevented received serious attention during the early 1960s under the Kennedy administration. In 1962, the President's Panel on Mental Retardation established the goal of reducing the incidence of mental retardation by 50 percent by the year 2000. Panel members believed this could be accomplished if current knowledge and technology were utilized in the prevention of mental retardation. Since that time, largely through federal support, significant progress has been made regarding the systematic prevention of mental retardation and other handicapping conditions. Much remains to be done, however, if a 50 percent reduction is to be achieved. In some situations, the prevention of mental retardation is a realistic and attainable goal; in most situations, the effects of mental retardation at least can be mitigated.

Prevention often is described as "primary" (preventing the birth of a retarded child), "secondary" (identification, with appropriate intervention, of infants at risk for mental retardation), or "tertiary" (the use of education, stimulation, medical or social services to reduce further handicaps). In the "primary" category, usually "high-risk" mothers must be identified for appropriate intervention, while "secondary" and "tertiary" preventive measures more often are directed toward children who are mentally retarded or at risk for mental retardation. (For excellent reviews of preventive agendas and strategies, see Alexander et al., 1981; Baroff, 1974; Crocker, 1982; Eklund, 1983, 1984, 1985; Johnston & Magrab, 1976; Milunsky, 1975).

## Primary Prevention

Probably the most important preventive measure against mental retardation is good prenatal care which ideally begins before pregnancy. Women should know their health status; they should be advised as to the harmful effects of tobacco, alcohol, drugs, and noxious substances in the environment. They should be informed about risks to the unborn baby if they have such health problems as diabetes, heart conditions, epilepsy, RH − blood type, and hypertension. Some should avoid pregnancy if possible and, if pregnancy occurs, be made aware of the options to terminate pregnancy. Women with PKU (Lenke & Levy, 1980), and women with mental retardation of unknown etiology (Lubs & Maes, 1977), for example, are at high risk for producing retarded or malformed babies. As a preventive measure, certain "high-risk" women should be counseled to delay pregnancy (Berg & Emanuel, 1983). This is especially true for teenagers, who, as a group, are at greater risk for producing very low birthweight babies (VLWB) and are at risk for all types of health problems for themselves and their babies.

Perinatal intensive care for the low birthweight premature infant (< 1,000 to 1,500 grams) has reduced the mortality rates of these infants and undoubtedly has been a factor in the prevention of mental retardation for many of those who survive (Berger, Gillings, & Siegel, 1976). However, intensive care brings with it many hardships to the family, both financially and emotionally. Among babies under 1,500 grams, the mean length of time they remain in the nursery is more than 3 months and at a cost that surpasses $100,000. A study by Benfield, Leib and Reuter (1976) found that parents of children in regional intensive care units needed support and understanding, along with someone to help them understand their concerns and fears about the prognosis. More than 50 percent of these parents believed that their babies would die, and almost 60 percent said they were depressed.

Good nutrition for expectant mothers helps to reduce the incidence of underweight and premature babies and concomitantly helps to reduce the rates of mental retardation, cerebral palsy and other handicapping conditions. Along with maternal nutrition, the diet of the developing child is crucial to the prevention of many health problems. (In recognition of the relationship among poverty, poor nutrition, low birthweight and developmental problems, the U.S. Congress authorized the Special Supplemental Food Program for Women, Infants and Children (WIC) in 1972.) The program provides food supplements to low-income women and their children under age 5 who are at nutritional risk. Breast-feeding now is recognized as a means of preventing certain illnesses that can lead to mental retardation. Compared to bottle-fed babies, breast-fed babies have a lower incidence of respiratory and diarrheal diseases and are less likely to suffer from serious neonatal infections and allergies. Also, breast-feeding is thought to help facilitate the mother-child bonding process. (See *The Report of the Surgeon General's Workshop on Breast Feeding and Human Lactation,* 1984).

Finally, genetic counseling itself can be a genuine preventive measure, if provided by a properly trained professional. Such counseling for individuals and/or families at risk needs to include the furnishing of information regarding factors that increase risk, the nature of the disorder, the prognosis, and possible consequences of the disease in relation to family life.

### Secondary Prevention

In terms of secondary prevention of mental retardation, the field of genetics has made significant contributions, especially with regard to prenatal diagnosis and carrier detection. The prevention of some genetic disorders is now possible; several other disorders, if discovered in time, can be treated with a fair degree of success. The development of prenatal diagnostic methods such as amniocentesis, ultrasound, and radiologic examination has made it possible to identify chromosomal aberrations, certain inborn errors of metabolism and other congenital abnormalities in the fetus. Prenatal diagnosis currently is offered for two primary reasons: (1) to assure, as reliably as possible, that the unborn child does not have the condition for which it was tested and (2) to offer the parents the option to terminate the pregnancy if the fetus indeed is found to be affected. (At this writing, the option to terminate such a pregnancy still is available.) The following situations have been widely accepted as indicators for offering prenatal diagnosis:

1. The mother will be 35 years of age or older or the father will be 55 or older at the time of the child's birth.
2. Either parent has a previous child with Down syndrome or another chromosomal abnormality.
3. There is a history of a relative with a proven potentially heritable chromosomal anomaly or mental retardation.
4. The couple has had a history of two or more miscarriages or infertility.
5. Either parent carries a balanced chromosome rearrangement (inversion or translocation).
6. There is a history of congenital malformation in either parent or in a previous child.
7. There is a family history of a neural tube defect (e.g. spina bifida or anencephaly).
8. Both members of the couple are carriers for an autosomal recessive disorder (e.g. Tay-Sachs, sickle cell, thalassemia, or PKU).
9. The mother is a known or possible carrier for X-linked mental retardation with or without the fragile X.
10. Either parent is affected with or has been shown to carry the gene for an autosomal dominant condition (e.g. tuberous sclerosis or neurofibromatosis).
11. The mother is an insulin-dependent diabetic, requires medication for epilepsy or has a history of other potential teratogenic exposure (e.g. rubella, X-ray or certain drugs used during pregnancy).
12. The parents are consanguineous (blood-related).
13. There is reason to suspect fetal abnormality on the basis of other studies (ultrasound, maternal serum, alpha-fetoprotein, Rh titre). (Burney, Walker & Dumars, 1984, p. 5)

In addition to the above traditional uses of prenatal diagnosis, increasing attention now is being given to the possibility of using this procedure as the first step in prenatal treatment. Efforts at intrauterine surgical procedures for hydrocephalus or other conditions, special dietary treatment for certain metabolic errors, and administering drugs that will influence the fetus are being evaluated presently. These new techniques eliminate the need for abortion in some instances, as previously life-threatening or handicapping problems are diagnosed and treated at early stages of prenatal life.

Thus used, prenatal diagnosis has a broader preventive application that goes beyond the use of this method as a way to give a parent more information to be utilized in deciding whether or not to terminate a pregnancy when the test result has been unfavorable for the birth of a normal, healthy infant. Understanding this idea of a broader use of prenatal diagnosis makes it possible to see a usefulness in having such a test available for pregnant women who would not choose to have an abortion even if the fetus were found to be defective. For these women, having prior knowledge of a defect could give them time to prepare, at least to some degree, for the emotional and other consequences of having a child with a significant problem. It also could give both the family and health professionals time to arrange for specialized needed services in the community.

Another preventive strategy used in the field of genetics involves heterozygote screening to determine actual carriers of a genetic disease in order to learn which individuals and couples are at a greater risk for having affected children. At this time, a few disorders, such as Tay-Sachs and sickle cell anemia, can be detected. For this type of screening to be effective, the condition must occur frequently enough to make screening cost-effective.

Prevention also occurs through the screening of newborn infants for "PKU" and congenital hypothyroidism. These screening procedures are widespread, but screening for other metabolic abnormalities is not routinely done in some states, because the low incidence of the metabolic disorders in question does not justify the cost of the procedure involved.

A promising type of screening that is expected to be widely used in the future involves the screening for open spinal defects such as spina bifida. Pilot programs already have been conducted in the U.S. on the feasibility of nationwide testing for the presence of alpha-fetoprotein in the blood of women (see, for example, Gastel et al., 1980). The blood of a pregnant woman whose unborn baby has an open spinal defect may contain excessive amounts of a protein called alpha-fetoprotein. However, as with all tests, positive results need verification and further testing, including amniocentesis and ultrasonography.

## Tertiary Prevention

Tertiary prevention activities are intended to prevent complications or to minimize the long-term effects of mental retardation. The interdisciplinary programs of the University Affiliated Facilities (UAFs) are examples of such programs.[2] Through research, training, service and demonstration projects, the UAFs bring together a variety of disciplines to help handicapped individuals reach their full potential.

Several studies provide evidence that demonstrate the effectiveness of "early intervention" as a prevention activity (see, for example, Gordon, 1969; Hanson, 1977; Haskins, Finkelstein, & Stedman, 1978; Heber, 1971; Lazar & Darlington, 1982). "Early" means anytime from early infancy through ages 4 to 5 years. "Intervention" encompasses any program that "keeps the child's development within normal limits, increases developmental rates, prevents secondary effects of a disability, keeps a child out of an institution or helps the family function more adequately" (Johnson & Chamberlin, 1983, p. 17).

In recognition that a child with handicaps is a family affair, the more successful programs at the tertiary level not only have focused on the child's developmental skills but have given special attention to the parents, to their restricted social life, and to their stresses and coping skills. The work of Badger (1977) with the Cincinnati Maternal and Infant Care Project, in providing multidisciplinary and comprehensive services to adolescent mothers, stressed the importance of improving "mother competence" as a means of improving the developmental outcome of their children. The young mothers who participated in this program received training in order to foster their own children's sensorimotor, cognitive and language development in addition to being made aware of their children's health, nutritional, psychological and educational needs. Not all early intervention programs show favorable results (Piper & Pless, 1980). The Head Start movement of the 1960s received considerable criticism when follow-up data showed that many children in these programs later lost the intellectual gains they had made through preschool stimulation. With any program, however, success is dependent on the child and family circumstances, the nature of the intervention, the timing in the developmental period, and the duration and intensity of care.

At all levels of prevention, experts in the field of mental retardation have identified strategies that work. However, knowing how to prevent mental retardation is one thing, but actually putting this knowledge into practice is another matter. It now appears that the momentum gained during the "golden years" of mental retardation of the 1960s and 1970s may be lost during the 1980s because of major cuts in funding for such programs. Therefore, this author is not optimistic about reaching the goal of reducing mental retardation by 50 percent by the year 2000.

## IMPLICATIONS FOR SOCIAL WORK RESEARCH

If prevention programs are to be effective, research efforts are necessary. The handicapped have been the beneficiaries of research, but research for the handicapped has not kept pace with research in other more popular areas. Lack of funding is one reason, but a lack of interest may also contribute. However, a 1977 report of the *Ad Hoc Committee on Mental Retardation* set forth many encouraging recommendations regarding the support of research. This report gave special emphasis to the fact that almost nothing is known about the etiology of most individuals with mental retardation, especially that caused by environmental factors during prenatal, perinatal and postnatal periods. The same report stressed the need for more demographic information on people who are mentally retarded (i.e. their life span and life-style), particularly those who are not institutionalized. Furthermore, little is known about how they adjust to the larger community, even though recent years have seen massive deinstitutionalization and mainstreaming. Therefore, it is not well known what is actually happening to all the people who are mentally retarded and who are suddenly entering the mainstream of community life in large numbers. This whole area should be of great concern, not only to social workers but also to professionals in education and many other fields, since it seems clear that they from now on are going to be in society in a very new way.

As a social-behavioral science, social work should focus much more strongly on the understanding of mental retardation due to environmental influences — an area where relatively little research has been done. If the ultimate goal of research in the field of mental retardation and developmental disabilities is to reduce the occurrence of mental retardation, then social work research should focus on understanding the causes of the rising number of teenage pregnancies that all too often result in mental retardation and otherwise children who are handicapped. With regard to lessening the damage of mental retardation to individuals, families and communities, research relating to the link between retardation and delinquency appears appropriate. Again, social work would seem to be qualified for investigating this area of concern, since it is in a position to work with local family and juvenile courts which admittedly deal with a high proportion of children considered mentally retarded to some degree. Appropriate subjects for social work research would include the link between child abuse and retardation; the effects of various kinds of family care (natural parents, foster parents, group homes) on people who are retarded; and the impact of the birth of a child who is developmentally disabled on the family unit.

Much psychological and medical research already has been done on the intellectual and physical development of both normal and developmentally disabled children. However, definitive studies of the social development of the mentally retarded and of what might be done to stimulate their development in this area are in many instances yet to be undertaken. It is probably in the understanding of the development of social competence, the ability to survive in the work a day world, that social work can make its most worthwhile contribution. The development of such an instrument would be a very significant milestone in both the understanding and the management of developmental disabilities, since social inadequacy (the ability to function in the day-to-day community) presents perhaps the main problem of many retarded persons, at least in a practical sense. It is a problem with which the profession of social work has long been familiar, and, therefore, social workers should have unique qualifications for contributing to its solution. Such research necessarily deals with intangibles that do not readily lend themselves to standard methods of measurement; consequently, such investigations can be difficult and require a highly creative approach. When such research does yield successful results, however, the application of its findings can hold to a minimum the damaging effects of those handicapping conditions on the individual family and society.

## NOTES

1. An instructional manual (McGrath, O'Hara, & Thomas, 1978), developed by directors of social work in University Affiliated Facilities, recommends major areas of knowledge which could be useful to graduate students entering the field

of mental retardation. The recommended knowledge base includes: genetics and chromosomal disorders; prenatal and perinatal influences on growth and development; human growth and development; major sensory defects of childhood; specific handicapping conditions and implications for family life; interdisciplinary practice, policies, programs and services for the developmentally handicapped; and social implications of being handicapped. Also defined were the desired practice skills and attitudes to be incorporated into the learning experience.

2. University Affiliated Facilities (UAF) are programs established to (1) train personnel in the interdisciplinary approach to the delivery of services; (2) conduct research; and (3) provide exemplary services related to persons with developmental disabilities and other multiply handicapping conditions. There are 49 such centers in 38 states and the District of Columbia.

## Chapter Two

# THE ROLE OF THE MAJOR DISCIPLINES IN THE FIELD OF MENTAL RETARDATION

B ECAUSE MANY children who are mentally retarded have complicated, lifelong medical, social and educational needs, services for these children are provided most effectively in an interdisciplinary setting where the core disciplines include social work, nursing, medicine, and psychology. In addition, a wide range of other specialized services should be available (i.e. speech, hearing, physical therapy, dentistry, vision function, and nutrition). Each of these disciplines is concerned with a specific aspect of the individual's developmental/health status, and the interrelationship between these health conditions is the essence of the interdisciplinary approach to services.

This chapter examines the roles of the major disciplines called on to provide services to people with mental retardation and their families.

## SOCIAL WORK

The role of social work in the field of mental retardation is well established, although historically social work has shown little concern with the field of mental retardation, "allowing itself to be represented by a relatively small number of standard-bearers" (Horejsi, 1979, p. 40). In the field of mental retardation, the social worker is concerned with the family's response to the child's disability and with stresses or conflicts that may arise in the care and management of the child. Parents of handicapped children in many cases experience stress which can be long lasting but which changes as the child grows older. This stress, in turn, affects family functioning. It can cause marital conflict; it can prevent the accomplishment of the family's personal and social goals; it can cause tension among the siblings. Additionally, families need direction in acquiring services, assistance in gaining access to advocacy programs, information about the diagnosis and prognosis of the disorder, and help in educational and vocational planning. Family members often need to interact through formal and informal discussion groups with other parents of handicapped children, and they need programs that teach them how to implement home therapy and self-help programs. These needs all require a holistic approach to the child and the family. It goes without saying that these issues are very familiar to practitioners in the social work profession and are concepts of care that are essential principles of social work practice. From a practical standpoint, the role of social work in providing services to individuals who are mentally retarded is to offer assistance in three major areas: counseling, advocacy, and environmental assistance.

## Counseling

Counseling has a different focus from different disciplines, but from a social work perspective, it usually involves supportive help, crisis intervention or simply clarification of certain conditions related to the child's handicap. Counseling can be short-term or long-term, depending on the stability of the family, resources available, and the severity and chronicity of the problem.

Supportive counseling is needed when parents are emotionally overwhelmed by the stress often associated with the day-to-day care of a handicapped child. A review of the literature by Wolfensberger (1967) covers some of the problems that frequently confront such parents. He discusses a number of issues, including the emotional reaction of the family to the disorder, the adjustment of siblings, coping mechanisms, counseling techniques, and possible residential placement decisions. However, this investigator emphasizes that many families do adjust to the presence of a handicapped child in a very positive way and do not require in-depth counseling or psychotherapy.

Help in crisis situations is a frequent need of people with mental retardation and their families. The crisis may be precipitated by the diagnosis itself or may be the result of unexpected changes that occur in the life of an individual with handicaps.

Anticipatory guidance refers to the giving of information in order to reduce anxiety. For example, clarification of certain health or developmental conditions may be of great help in reducing anxiety. Furthermore, allowing parents to share their feelings (which often are feelings of inadequacy and self-blame) may aid them in making realistic plans for the future. Nevertheless, the chronic nature of mental retardation underscores the likelihood that counseling of some type will be required at some point in the life of an individual with mental retardation and/or the family.

## Advocacy

The need for a range of services which both directly support the person with handicaps and his family, as well as insure community responsibility for handicapped groups, is well documented (McGrath, O'Hara & Thomas, 1978). To obtain basic information about the different needs of the mentally retarded, the social work staff at the Sparks Center surveyed parents of 100 children with mental retardation. Table 1 lists the service needs as perceived by these parents (80 responses = 80% response rate).

TABLE 1

Service Needs As Perceived by Parents of Handicapped Children
N = 80

| Service | Expressed Need % |
| --- | --- |
| Special Education | 47 |
| Recreational Programs | 47 |
| Support Groups | 46 |
| Financial Aid | 46 |
| Preschool Education | 43 |
| Day Care Facilities | 42 |
| Training in Personal Care | 42 |
| Physical Therapy | 42 |
| Vocational Education | 41 |
| Medical Services | 38 |
| Family Counseling | 34 |
| Parent Training | 34 |
| Individual Counseling | 32 |
| Special Equipment | 30 |
| Infant Program | 24 |
| Residential Care | 22 |
| Genetic Counseling | 20 |
| Short-term Respite Care ( < 30 days) | 16 |
| Group Home Care | 14 |
| Long-term Respite Care ( > 30 days) | 9 |

Whatever services are required for individuals who are retarded, the coordination or the linkage of these services is basic to their success. The following statement by the President's Committee on Mental Retardation of 1972 still is true today: "Coordination is probably the most crucial factor in successful administration of mental retardation programs. This is so because mental retardation cannot be confined to any one health, education, rehabilitation or welfare program or any single disciplinary group. A total program must include a wide range of activities designed to confront the problem of mental retardation simultaneously from many vantage points." Social workers, long considered to be the liaison agents between families and community services, should have special qualifications to insure that these services are coordinated and to find realistic ways to meet the practical everyday needs of children with handicaps and their families.

Advocacy for services for the handicapped population is an ever-present issue, despite the fact that laws have been passed to assure that they have equal access to education, employment, financial aid, use of public facilities, and all other services available to the population at large. Major legislation was passed in 1975 (P.L. 94-142; see Chapter 3) with mandated provisions of appropriate free educational resources for children with handicaps; however, more than 10 years later, many professionals including educators still are not fully aware of the rights of the handicapped. In those cases where legal and professional advocacy services are indicated, parents should be referred to the state's protection and advocacy agency.

## Environmental Assistance

Social workers always have worked with families of individuals with handicaps. In the past, these efforts frequently have been directed primarily towards helping parents deal with the emotional aspects of having a child with handicaps. This is a proper concern and social workers should not abandon it. Some social workers, however, may have a tendency to see parents of the handicapped somehow as "patients" in their own right. This concept rapidly is losing validity among most social workers who have had broad experience with the developmentally disabled and who are impressed with how healthy (in terms of functioning) many families are, especially given the multiple difficulties faced by many of them.

In view of such circumstances, social workers may need to begin looking at families differently. Families must be seen increasingly as the "worker's co-therapists" who can be valuable allies in making the day-to-day life of the disabled child happy and productive. Thus, the oldest role of social work, to enhance social functioning, comes to the forefront again. This enhancement is one of the most significant contributions the social work profession can make toward improving the quality of life for individuals who are mentally retarded.

## NURSING

The influence of nursing on the field of mental retardation is best demonstrated through its contribution in programs of early intervention and work with high-risk infants. The nursing role, however, may vary according to the type of setting in which the intervention takes places (e.g. day-care centers, public health agencies, and/or schools).

At many University Affiliated Facilities, the nursing division, as part of the interdisciplinary team, works closely with disabled infants and their families in order to promote each child's development. The purpose of these programs is to teach parents various therapy and play techniques which can be incorporated into home programs. Additionally, parents learn to deal with such areas as health promotion, toileting, feeding, language stimulation, and motor development.

A comprehensive guide for nurses in the assessment of the growth and development of children with developmental disabilities is provided by Steele (1985). This manual, *Nursing Assessment of Young Children Vulnerable to Developmental Disabilities,* covers a broad range of assessments, including physical, cognitive, behavioral, and self-help areas. Other screening procedures performed by nursing concentrate on the developmental, hearing, vision, and speech capacities of children. The Denver Developmental Screening Test is one example of an assessment tool used for children from the age of 1 month to 6 years. This test provides information about the child's functioning and personal/social, fine motor, adaptive, gross motor and language skills. In addition to the Denver Series (Denver I Screening Test, Denver Articulation Screening Exam, Denver Audiometric Screening Test), other screening instruments are available that are inexpensive and easy to administer.

The focus on nursing intervention comprises teaching self-help skills to the children when age appropriate, and teaching parents these skills so that they can encourage their children to become as independent as possible. In the diagnostic and treatment process, nursing is recognized as an integral part of the interdisciplinary team.

## MEDICINE

Physical illnesses and handicapping conditions tend to be a part of mental retardation. The more severe the retardation, the stronger the possibility of secondary impairments. Individuals with mental retardation seem especially susceptible to respiratory illness; they have a high incidence of seizures; some suffer multiple physical handicaps; and some have visual, speech and hearing impairments. In general, a broad range of both acute and chronic medical problems can be expected. Consequently, children with mental retardation will require diagnostic and treatment services from a number of medical specialties including genetics, pediatrics, neurology, orthopedics, opthalmology, neonatology, and child psychiatry. Specialists in these areas are called upon most frequently to provide care at various developmental stages in the lives of children with mental retardation. A booklet by Richmond, Tarjan and Mendelsohn (1976) provides information for medical practitioners regarding the diagnosis of mental retardation and its treatment and medical management. These authors emphasize the importance of ongoing assessments.

## PSYCHOLOGY

The role of psychology in the diagnosis and treatment of mental retardation has been well defined. This discipline traditionally evaluates the child's intellectual, social, and emotional status; provides therapy to alleviate behavior and/or emotional problems; and offers assistance to educators in providing services designed to improve the child's fundamental academic skills. Some of the tests administered to infants and preschoolers by psychologists include:

1. Bayley Scales of Infant Development (Psychological Corporation, 1969);
2. Cattell Infant Intelligence Scale (Psychological Corporation, 1940);
3. Wechsler Preschool and Primary Scale of Intelligence (Psychological Corporation, 1967).

Other special tests can evaluate the child's emotional status, social competence, visual-motor ability, language skills, and achievement level. In addition, other testing instruments have been developed to evaluate children with specific physical impairments. One such test is the Hiskey-Nebraska Test of Learning Aptitude (Union College Press, 1966), which is standardized for deaf and hearing-impaired children ages 3 to 16.

The psychologist often is called upon to provide a type of therapy directed toward changing or modifying inappropriate or uncontrollable behavior. Central to the concept of behavior therapy is the premise that inappropriate behavior is "learned" and thus can be "unlearned." This approach, sometimes called "operant conditioning," is employed to facilitate such tasks as toilet training, behavior management, and weight control. Though some criticism has been directed toward this method of therapy, it has been acclaimed highly by many professionals in the field of behavioral science and special education. This technique of behavior management can be taught to parents, thus providing an opportunity for them to take more active roles in their child's development.

## SPEECH AND HEARING

Communication involves speech, language, and hearing, all of which are interrelated. Communication disorders comprise a broad range of receptive and expressive disabilities fairly common among children with developmental disabilities. These disabilities can be classified as psychological, physiological, or neurological. Thus stuttering might be considered behavioral (psychological) or neurological. On the other hand, speech defects associated with cleft lip/palate would be considered physiological, as they are the result of oral structural defects.

Some genetic disorders manifest severe speech, language, and hearing problems, frequently noted as one component of a syndrome. For example, in Down syndrome, delayed speech usually is a primary component of the patient's disability; similarly, hearing defects are associated with an inherited disorder called Waardenburg syndrome. In summary, a wide range of communication disorders, varied in both severity and type, is seen among children with developmental delays. One child with developmental aphasia may have no speech, while another child with the same disorder may display only mild articulation problems.

When a child's speech is delayed, the presence or absence of a hearing impairment should be determined by an audiologist, who evaluates hearing sensitivity and discrimination as well as middle-ear functioning. The true incidence of hearing loss among children probably is higher than might be anticipated. Also, the criteria for hearing impairment vary from study to study. Although the incidence of severe hearing impairment is about 1 in 1,000 births, some measurable hearing loss probably occurs in about 1 in 800 births. Moreover, many children may develop hearing loss in early childhood due to disease or to a degenerative process.

Hearing sensitivity impairments can be defined as being (1) conductive (involving the external or middle ear), (2) sensorineural (involving the inner ear or auditory nerve), or (3) mixed (involving a combination of conductive and sensorineural). The causes of hearing loss are many; such loss can result from accidents, ear infections, prenatal and postnatal infections, noise, diseases, genetic errors, prematurity, birth defects, and teratogenic agents.

Detection of a hearing impairment during infancy is difficult using both subjective and/or objective tests. Hearing sensitivity, however, can be determined to some extent. In assessing young and/or multiply handicapped children, the audiologist often relies on behavioral observation techniques. Localization to sound sources is utilized for children between the developmental ages of 6 months and 2 years with usual reinforced techniques. Play audiometry frequently is used with children between the ages of 2 and 5, while standard audiometric testing techniques can be used with most children beyond age 4.

A procedure called "operant conditioning" is effective with children who are multiply handicapped. This approach, however, requires considerable time, as reinforcers are used to maintain or modify responses to sound. Objective electrophysiological techniques (brainstem audiometry) are utilized to assess those who do not give reliable behavioral responses. Impedence audiometry is a technique that involves assessment of the middle-ear system in order to determine if the middle ear is functioning normally. Audiologically, children with developmental delays are more difficult to evaluate. They require more time than "normal" children in the evaluation process, and often test results are only tentative.

When a hearing impairment is diagnosed, a hearing aid sometimes is recommended. One should be aware, however, that hearing aids cannot correct sound-discrimination problems, nor are they routinely fitted on children with central auditory disorders. In recommending a hearing aid, an audiologist considers (1) the type of loss, (2) the degree of loss, (3) the tolerance of the ear for loud noises, (4) the maturation level of the child, and (5) the degree of benefit for the child.

Some debate continues as to the best method of teaching children who are severely hearing-impaired to communicate and to understand communication. The debate concerns the utilization of a strictly oral approach versus a manual approach versus a total communication approach. Proponents of total communication advocate a combination of oral and manual methods, utilizing auditory training, lip reading, sign manual and finger spelling, as well as facial expressions.

For speech/language evaluation, various tests are used to determine the individual's receptive and expressive language as well as his/her articulation and oral-motor abilities. Currently, many tests are available to assess the child's sound production skills (i.e. articulation). The Peabody Picture Vocabulary Test (revised) (Dunn & Dunn, 1981) and the Test for Auditory Comprehension of Language (revised) frequently are used as formal measures of receptive language functioning (Carrow-Wookfold, 1985). Developmental Sentence Scoring (Lee, 1974) and Assigning Structural Stage (Miller, 1979) can be utilized to determine level of expressive language functioning. In recent years speech-language pathologists increasingly have become concerned not only with the child's syntax and semantics but also with the pragmatics of language (i.e. the manner in which the child uses language). Within the past 10 years, increasing emphasis has been placed on correcting receptive and expressive language defects. Over the years speech/language pathologists have focused primarily on articulation remediation; they have tended to place a higher priority on receptive and expressive language skills. One should note, however, that any therapeutic programming should be individualized around specific problem areas.

## PHYSICAL THERAPY

The major function of physical therapy with people who are developmentally disabled is to improve posture and locomotion which often are seen in conjunction with mental retardation, disorders caused by brain damage (i.e. cerebral palsy), and disorders caused by spinal cord damage (i.e. spina bifida).

Gross motor development involves the gradual acquisition of movement skills (i.e. reaching, walking, and running), whereas fine motor function refers to such activities as grasping or writing. Deficits in both gross and fine motor development are especially evident in children with spina bifida and with cerebral palsy in its severe form, but motor problems may not be as apparent in some individuals with mental retardation. However, certain individuals with mental retardation do manifest rather obvious motor problems (i.e. the Down syndrome patient, who frequently has decreased muscle tone and poor coordination). With varying degrees of mental retardation have some type of motor delay (i.e. decreased or increased muscle tone, poor reflexes, poor coordination, difficulty in balancing, and lack of strength). Some individuals may show delays in all areas of physical development, and in fact a delay in motor development may be the first clue that the child is mentally retarded. For successful treatment of individuals with developmental delays, "the physical therapist must begin treatment at an early age, provide an individualized program to improve the function of each child and/or his family, involve the family in home management, continually re-evaluate the potential for further development, and correlate treatment with programs of other treating disciplines." (Harryman, 1976, p. 188).

## DENTISTRY

People who are mentally retarded usually have a high incidence of poor dental hygiene, periodontal disease, and malocclusion (poor bite). Severe gingival (gum) disease sometimes is seen when an individual is taking medication for seizure control. Some drugs used in seizure control can cause enlargement of the gums and gum disease if dental hygiene is poor. Sometimes it is necessary to remove surgically the excessive amount of gingival tissue in order to restore proper chewing function of the teeth and to maintain good oral hygiene.

Malocclusion or orthodontic problems can be the result of a developmental facial discrepancy. For example, Apert syndrome is manifested in one way by deficient mid-facial growth; the results of this growth gives the appearance of a protruding lower jaw plus a very small upper jaw.

Cleft lip and/or palate is a severe handicapping condition which can occur independently or with certain chromosomal disorders. Because such cases involve severe speech and dental problems, they should be managed by an interdisciplinary team of specialists.

The quality of dental hygiene in persons with mental retardation always has been a major problem. The high incidence of periodontal disease in this population probably is related to the fact that most individuals with handicaps cannot provide for their own dental health needs; in general, they do not follow good dietary practices. The responsibility of good dental care usually is left up to the parents or attendants. Members of the health team who have constant contact with the mentally retarded must be aware of the importance of dental heath care as part of the total health picture.

Generally, the handicapped do not receive comprehensive dental care. Several factors are recognized by the dental profession as deterrents to obtaining adequate dental care for the handicapped. These include (1) insufficient student training within the dental schools; (2) the reluctance of dentists to treat these patients in their offices; (3) poor access to dental offices because of architectural barriers and transportation problems; (4) a low priority for dental health care because of other burdens requiring considerable attention; and (5) inadequate financial resources to cover the expense of dental treatment (Thornton, 1983).

## VISION FUNCTION[1]

To illustrate some of the visual problems associated with mental retardation, three conditions are discussed: (1) cerebral palsy, (2) mucopolysaccharidoses, and (3) Down syndrome. Each condition has its own set of eye signs which are closely, but not exclusively, associated with the condition.

### Cerebral Palsy (CP)

Approximately 31 percent of individuals with cerebral palsy (CP) display significant visual problems. These visual problems usually are the "extremes" of much rarer conditions found in the general populace.

To illustrate this point, the condition known as strabismus (a manifest eye turn where one eye may turn in, out, up or down while the other eye fixes on an object of regard) is found in 69 percent of the CP population with visual problems. This is more than a fivefold increase when compared to the general population where only about 4 out of 100 will exhibit strabismus.

Other visual conditions are in the same general disproportion. More than 64 percent of the population with CP manifests significant refractive errors (need for spectacles); this means that among 100 mentally retarded individuals with CP, 18 will need a significant spectacle correction. In that same group of 100, 13 will display the condition known as nystagmus. Nystagmus is an involuntary oscillation of the eye which is usually in a rhythmic pendular pattern. It always signals a significant decrease in vision and is usually congenital. Although there have been attempts to eliminate nystagmus through the use of biofeedback, the techniques have been strictly experimental and no attempts have been made to adapt these techniques to the mentally retarded.

## Mucopolysaccharidoses (MPS)

The second condition, mucopolysaccharidoses (MPS), generally is characterized as a family of disease entities whose etiology is genetic in origin. This disorder results in the abnormal accumulation of mucopolysaccharides in various tissues, including the eye.

The major eye signs include, but are not limited to, corneal clouding, retinal degeneration, and glaucoma. Corneal clouding seldom is evident at birth but develops over the first year of life. Retinal degeneration usually follows soon after. The degeneration, in part, may be due to the presence of form deprivation resulting from the corneal clouding. It also may be due to the presence of a genetic defect. The third major sign for many of the MPS family is glaucoma. Glaucoma (increased pressure inside the eyeball) is caused by the mucopolysaccharides' blocking the drainage of fluid (aqueous) within the eye so that pressure gradually increases. This results in the death of the light-carrying visual cells — the rods and cones. Infants and children who appear to have a hazy or "ground glass" appearance of their corneae should be genetically tested for MPS, and, if possible, the specific form should be diagnosed. Since the MPS family has progressive changes, prompt diagnosis may provide an indication of early visual complications.

## Down Syndrome

Down syndrome is the best known of the syndromes which involve mental retardation. Every Down child needs a visual examination. Besides the characteristic appearance of prominent epicanthal folds (40%), upward-slanting eyes (44%), and eyelid pathology (38-40%), other more serious visual signs may be present. These can be (1) keratoconus, (2) high refractive error, (3) strabismus, and (4) cataracts. Keratoconus is a corneal condition in which a portion of the cornea weakens and becomes "cone" shaped. Severe cases can lead to corneal penetration and the subsequent loss of an eye. High refractive error often is associated with Down syndrome and normally necessitates wearing of spectacles. Usually these children are found to be significantly myopic (nearsighted), although they may be significantly hyperopic (farsighted). In either situation, glasses prescribed at a relatively early age may prevent further complications such as strabismus or amblyopia ("lazy eye"). Strabismus is extremely common in this population. Most references indicate about 2 percent of the general population has strabismus. In Down children about 38 percent manifest strabismus with about 10-to-1 chance of exhibiting an inward turn of one or both eyes versus an outward turn of the eye.

The illustrations noted represent only three groups of children who may be mentally retarded and also exhibit significant visual anomalies. These data make it apparent that all children with mental retardation should have complete eye examinations. However, eye examinations must answer more than just the level of acuity for these children. They also must evaluate the refractive status (the need for glasses), the binocular status (the ability to use both eyes together), and the eye health. Yet, the single most important item in each examination often is overlooked and must be addressed: Is this child's visual capabilities sufficient to meet his mental capacity? One must weigh this potential with the child's sensory ability, and in situations which warrant the effort, every attempt must be made to provide for the visual welfare of the mentally retarded child.


## NUTRITION[2]

Nutrition plays an important role in the growth, development, and health of children who are developmentally disabled, just as it does for normal children. Nutrition's role involves both prevention and treatment. Achieving good nutritional status is more difficult for the developmentally disabled child and relates particularly to the severity of the disability.

The role of nutrition in the prevention of developmental disabilities involves providing adequate nutrients and energy during the perinatal period and infancy up to age 2 or 3 to ensure adequate growth and development of the brain and neurological system.

Extensive research has been done in the area of nutrition and brain cell development utilizing animal models followed by retrospective studies of children in underdeveloped countries exposed to undernutrition for extended periods of time. Inadequate intake of protein and energy for extended periods of time from the last trimester of pregnancy through 14 months of age can cause a decrease in the number of cells (Rozovski & Winick, 1979). If the nutritional insult occurs after 14 months of age, cell size decreases.

The second and more obvious role of nutrition in the prevention of developmental disabilities involves inborn errors of metabolism. The best-known metabolic error which causes mental retardation and developmental disabilities when untreated is phenylketonuria (PKU). This particular disorder, discovered in 1934, makes early treatment difficult because of the necessity for finding a replacement for milk.

PKU is caused by either a lack of, or the absence of, the enzyme necessary for breaking down the essential amino acid (a protein-building block) to the normal metabolic pathway. It requires treatment by the provision of a special formula low in phenylalanine. Recently, new formulas have been developed which are totally lacking in phenylalanine. Additional treatment involves providing foods limited in phenylalanine content (i.e. fruits, vegetables, cereals, and fats).

Other inborn errors which can result in developmental disabilities and mental retardation if untreated include galactosemia, tyrosinemia, homocystinuria, arginiosuccinic aciduria, maple syrup urine disease, and isovaleric aciduria. Many other inborn errors have been identified, and dietary treatment either has been developed or is under way. As a general rule, the limiting factor which may be an amino acid, carbohydrate, or fat is restricted in the dietary management (Nyhan, 1981).

The second role for nutrition requires providing adequate nutrients, protein, fat, carbohydrates, vitamins, minerals, and water for meeting the nutritional needs of the child or adult with developmental disabilities. The energy value of food is achieved through consumption of protein, fats, and carbohydrates. Energy needs of the body are determined by the basic needs: heartbeat, circulation, respiration, and muscle contraction, plus growth and activity.

Children with developmental delays have the same qualitative nutritional needs as all children and may have greater needs because of their handicaps (Caldwell, 1982). Some research indicates, however, that quantitative nutritional needs may be less for certain conditions such as Down syndrome, spina bifida, Turner syndrome, and Klinefelter syndrome. The basic metabolic energy needs may be lower for individuals with these conditions; they also may have a slower growth rate and lessened physical activity. When their food intake meets the recommendations for a normal, moderately active individual, these individuals often become overweight and later obese (Palmer & Ekvall, 1978).

Early identification of weight when it is disproportionate to height is an important component of the care of a developmentally disabled individual. Referral to a registered dietitian for a complete assessment of their nutritional status and development of a weight control program is needed as soon as possible to prevent further weight gain. Usually, a behavioral and exercise component is necessary in achieving weight reduction (Wodarski, 1985). Obesity is a difficult problem to solve for the child who is developmentally disabled, since food provision is often symbolic with love in the perception of the parent.

Other handicapping conditions such as cerebral palsy and neurological damage may result in undernutrition precipitated by feeding problems. Some of these problems result in lack of mouth, head, and truck control; lack of sitting balance; and inability to bend the hips, to grasp, and to self-feed, hampering the eating process (Wodarski, 1985). As a consequence, nutrient and energy needs are not met and the child fails to gain weight, grow adequately in length, fight off infectious diseases, or have sufficient energy for various therapeutic procedures.

To ensure adequate nutrition, food must be provided in a form appropriate for the individual's stage of oral-motor development. The skills of the registered dietitian are needed to recommend supplemental beverages and food which will enhance the caloric and protein content of the diet.

Medications frequently are prescribed for this population. Anticonvulsant drugs such as phenobarbital, phenytein, and prinidone have been found to decrease serum levels of folic acid and vitamin D. Stimulant drugs such as dextroamphetamine often depress appetite and should be given after meals are eaten (Wodarski, 1985).

Constipation is another side effect of anticonvulsant drugs and tranquilizers; it also occurs in disorders such as spina bifida. The problem is confounded by lack of mobility and exercise. Increasing the fiber and fluid content of the diet has reduced the need for laxatives (Wodarski, 1985).

In summary, optimal nutrition is essential for the health and well-being of every person. Children with developmental disabilities have more difficulty acquiring adequate nutrients and kilocalories. Consequently, nutrition assessment leading to nutritional care is an important part of total planning for the developmentally disabled child.

## NOTES

1. The section on Vision Function was written by Michael D. Wesson, O.D., M.S., Director, Division of Vision Function, Chauncey Sparks Center for Developmental and Learning Disorders, University of Alabama at Birmingham.
2. The section on "Nutrition" was written by Harriet H. Cloud, M.S., R.D., Director, Division of Nutrition, Chauncey Sparks Center for Developmental and Learning Disorders, University of Alabama at Birmingham.

## Chapter Three

# LEGAL PROVISIONS FOR THE MENTALLY RETARDED/DEVELOPMENTALLY DISABLED[1]

## INTRODUCTION

THE TOPIC OF legal provisions for individuals who are mentally retarded/developmentally disabled is an extremely broad one. (In this chapter, the term "developmentally disabled" includes the mentally retarded.) Issues arise from the time frame of before birth until after death of the individual. Issues already litigated range from medical care of the fetus to every service and right afforded across the entire spectrum of life.

The purpose of this chapter is to provide a brief overview of the legal provisions for the area of mental retardation/developmental disabilities. The manner in which social workers approach legal issues will be guided in large measure by agency policy, job description, and respective state legislation. Therefore, the source of generic provisions of services and rights for individuals with these disabilities is federal legislation. Federal legislation directly influences services provided in all comprehensive, social, educational, and rehabilitation programs. This chapter will focus on these four areas.

The reader should remember that individuals with developmental disabilities have the same rights as all other individuals. Historically, individuals with developmental disabilities have been denied those rights and services provided normal persons. Consequently, they now have additional rights guaranteed by federal legislation to ensure due process and equal protection in receiving services via governmental sources.

## COMPREHENSIVE PROVISIONS

Congress found that a need existed to place the responsibility of safeguarding the rights of the developmentally disabled under one regulatory agency. The Department of Health and Human Services was selected for this task.

## Developmentally Disabled Assistance and Bill of Rights Act of 1984

Congressional intent to streamline services to the developmentally disabled is detailed in the Developmentally Disabled Assistance and Bill of Rights Acts (DDA) of 1984 (Public Law [P.L.] 98-527).

### *Purpose of DDA*

The general intent and specific provisions are as follows:

(b)(1) It is the overall purpose of this title to assist states to assure that persons with developmental disabilities receive the care, treatment, and other services necessary to enable them to achieve their maximum potential through a system which coordinates, monitors, plans, and evaluates those services and which ensures the protection of the legal and human rights of persons with developmental disabilities.

(2) The specific purposes of this title are—

(A) to assist in the provision of comprehensive services to persons with developmental disabilities, with priority to those persons whose needs cannot be covered or otherwise met under the Education of All Handicapped Children Act, the Rehabilitation Act of 1973 (29 U.S.C.S. § 701 et seq.) or other health, education, or welfare programs;

(B) to assist states in appropriate planning activities;

(C) to make grants to states and public and private, non-profit agencies to establish model programs, to demonstrate innovative habilitation techniques, and to train professional and paraprofessional personnel with respect to providing services to persons with developmental disabilities;

(D) to make grants to university-affiliated facilities to assist them in administering and operating demonstration facilities for the provision of services to persons with developmental disabilities, and interdisciplinary training programs for personnel needed to provide specialized services for these persons; and

(E) to make grants to support a system in each state to protect the legal and human rights of all persons with developmental disabilities. (42 U.S.C.S. § 6000[b])

## Definitions

To assist in clarifying terminology used in DDA (1984), the following definitions are provided:

(7) The term "developmental disability" means a severe, chronic disability of a person which—

(A) is attributable to a mental or physical impairment or combination of mental and physical impairments;

(B) is manifested before the person attains age twenty-two;

(C) is likely to continue indefinitely;

(D) results in substantial functional limitations in three or more of the following areas of major life activity: (i) self-care, (ii) receptive and expressive language, (iii) learning, (iv) mobility, (v) self-direction, (vi) capacity for independent living, and (vii) economic self-sufficiency;

(E) reflects the person's need for a combination and sequence of special, interdisciplinary, or generic care, treatment, or other services which are lifelong or of extended duration and are individually planned and coordinated.

(8) (A) The term "services for persons with developmental disabilities" means priority services (as defined in subparagraph B) and any other specialized services or special adaptations of generic services for persons with developmental disabilities, including in these services the diagnosis, evaluation, treatment, personal care, day care, domiciliary care, special living arrangements, training, education, sheltered employment, recreation, counseling of the individual with such disability and of his family, protective and other social and sociolegal services, information and referral services, follow-along services, and transportation services necessary to assure delivery of services to persons with developmental disabilities.

(B) The term "priority services" means case management services (as defined in subparagraph C), child development services (as defined in subparagraph D), alternative community living arrangement services (as defined in subparagraph E), and non-vocational social-developmental services (as defined in subparagraph F).

(C) The term "case management services" means such services to persons with developmental disabilities as will assist them in gaining access to needed social, medical, educational, and other services; and such terms include—

(i) follow-along services which ensure, through a continuing relationship, lifelong if necessary, between an agency or provider and a person with a developmental disability and the person's immediate relatives or guardians, that the changing needs of the person and the family are recognized and appropriately met; and

(ii) coordination services which provide to persons with developmental disabilities support, access to (and coordination of) other services, information on programs and services, and monitoring of the person's progress.

(D) The term "child development services" means such services as will assist in the prevention, identification, and alleviation of developmental disabilities in children, and includes (i) early intervention services, (ii) counseling and training of parents, (iii) early identification of developmental disabilities, and diagnosis and evaluation of such developmental disabilities.

(E) The term "alternative community living arrangement services" means such services as will assist persons with developmental disabilities in maintaining suitable residential arrangements in the community, and includes in-house services (such as personal aides and attendants and other domestic assistance and supportive services), family support services, foster care services, group living services, respite care, and staff training, placement, and maintenance services. (42 U.S.C.S. § 6001)

## Congressional Findings

Congress made the following findings with respect to the rights of individuals with developmental disabilities:

(1) Persons with developmental disabilities have a right to appropriate treatment, services, and habilitation for such disabilities.

(2) The treatment, services, and habilitation for a person with developmental disabilities should be designed to maximize the developmental potential of the person and should be provided in the setting that is least restrictive of the person's personal liberty.

(3) The federal government and the states both have an obligation to assure that public funds are not provided to any institutional or other residential program for persons with developmental disabilities that—

(A) does not provide treatment, services, and habilitation which is appropriate to the needs of such persons; or

(B) does not meet the following minimum standards:

(i) Provision of a nourishing, well-balanced daily diet to the persons with developmental disabilities being served by the program.

(ii) Provision to such persons of appropriate and sufficient medical and dental services.

(iii) Prohibition of the use of physical restraint on such persons unless absolutely necessary and prohibition of the use of such restraint as a punishment or as a substitute for a habilitation program.

(iv) Prohibition on the excessive use of chemical restraints on such persons and the use of such restraints as punishment or as a substitute for a habilitation program or in quantities that interfere with services, treatment, or habilitation for such persons.

(v) Permission for close relatives of such persons to visit them at reasonable hours without prior notice.

(vi) Compliance with adequate fire and safety standards as may be promulgated by the secretary.

(4) All programs for persons with developmental disabilities should meet standards which are designed to assure the most favorable possible outcome for those served, and—

(A) in the case of residential programs serving persons in need of comprehensive health-related, habilitative, or rehabilitative services, which are at least equivalent to those standards applicable to intermediate care facilities for the mentally retarded promulgated in regulations of the secretary on January 17, 1974 (39 Fed. Reg. pt. II), as appropriate when taking into account the size of the institutions and the service delivery arrangements of the facilities of the program:

(B) in the case of other residential programs for persons with developmental disabilities, which assure that care is appropriate to the needs of the persons being served by such progarms, assure that the persons admitted to facilities of such programs are persons whose needs can be met through services provided by such facilities, and assure that the facilities under such programs provide for the human care of the residents of the facilities, are sanitary, and protect their rights; and

(C) in the case of non-residential programs, which assure the care provided by such programs is appropriate to the persons served by the programs.

The rights of persons with developmental disabilities described in findings made in this section are in addition to any constitutional or other rights otherwise afforded to all persons. (42 U.S.C.S. § 6010).

### Habilitation Plan

As a condition for receiving an allotment, each state must ensure that each developmentally disabled person provided service has a habilitation plan which meets the following requirements under DDA (1984):

(1) The plan shall be in writing.

(2) The plan shall be developed jointly by (A) a representative or representatives of the program primarily responsible for delivering or coordinating the delivery of services to the person for whom the plan is established, and (B) where appropriate, such person's parents or guarandian or other representative.

(3) The plan shall contain a statement of the long-term habilitation goals for the person and the intermediate habilitation objectives relating to the attainments of such goals. Such objectives shall be stated specifically and in sequence and shall be expressed in behavioral or other terms that provide measurable indices of progress. The plan shall (A) describe how the objectives will be achieved and the barriers that might interfere with the achievement of them, (B) state objective criteria and an evaluation procedure and schedule for determining whether such objectives and goals are being achieved, and (C) provide for a program coordinator who will be responsible for the implementation of the plan.

(4) The plan shall contain a statement (in readily understandable form) of specific habilitation services to be provided, shall identify each agency which will deliver such services, shall describe the personnel (and their qualifications) necessary for the provision of such services, and shall specify the date of the initiation of each service to be provided and the anticipated duration of each such service.

(5) The plan shall specify the role and objectives of all parties to the implementation of the plan.

> (c) Annual review. Each habilitation plan shall be reviewed at least annually by the agency primarily responsible for the delivery of services to the person for whom the plan was established or responsible for the coordination of the delivery of services to such person. In the course of the review, such person and the person's parents or guardian or other representa-

tive shall be given an opportunity to review such plan and to participate in its revision. (42 U.S.C.S. § 6011 [b], [c])

### *Advocacy Program*

Congress found a need for developmentally disabled persons to have protection and advocacy of individual rights and documented such in DDA (1984) as follows:

(a) In order for a state to receive an allotment under part C (42 U.S.C.S. § 6061 et seq.)

(1) the state must have in effect a system to protect and advocate the rights of persons with developmental disabilities,

(2) such system must (A) have the authority to pursue legal, administraive, and other appropriate remedies to insure the protection of the rights of such persons who are receiving treatment, services, or habilitation within the state, (B) not be administered by the state planning council, and (C) be independent of any agency which provides treatment, services, or habilitation to persons with developmental disabilities, and

(3) the state must submit to the secretary in a form prescribed by the secretary in regulations (A) a report, not less often than once every three years, describing the system, and (B) an annual report describing the activities carried out under the system and any changes made in the system during the previous year. (42 U.S.C.S. § 6012 [a])

The reader should note that DDA (1984) is an act to streamline services and clarify rights but is not a funding source.

## SOCIAL PROVISIONS

Congress has provided for the social, domestic, and general welfare needs of the developmentally disabled through legislation on adoption, assistance to foster families, child abuse prevention, housing and rental supplements, and community-based care.

### Adoption Assistance and Child Welfare Act of 1980

The Adoption Assistance and Child Welfare Act of 1980 (P.L. 96-272) was written to strengthen existing programs of foster care, to establish a program of adoption assistance, and to strengthen services to families with dependent children. Although services are not limited to atypical youngsters, the developmentally disabled comprise a high incidence of the population receiving services under this act.

### State Plan

Each state is required under P.L. 96-272 to submit a plan for foster care and adoption assistance which in part:

(9) provides that where any agency of the state has reason to believe that the home or institution in which a child resides whose care is being paid for in whole or in part with funds provided under this part or part B of this title is unsuitable for the child because of the neglect, abuse, or exploitation of such child, it shall bring such condition to the attention of the appropriate court or law enforcement agency. . .

(12) provides for granting an opportunity for a fair hearing before the state agency to any individual whose claim for benefits available pursuant to this part is denied or is not acted upon with reasonable promptness. . .

(14) provides (A) specific goals (which shall be established by state law on or before October 1, 1982) for each fiscal year (commencing with the fiscal year which begins on October 1, 1983) as to the maximum number of children (in absolute numbers or as a percentage of all children in foster care with respect to whom assistance under the plan is provided during such year) who, at any time during the year, will remain in foster care after having been in such care for a period in excess of twenty-four months, and (B) a description of the steps which will be taken by the state to achieve such goals. . .

(15) effective October 1, 1983, provides that, in each case, reasonable efforts will be made (A) prior to the placement of a child in foster care, to prevent or eliminate the need for removal of the child from his home, and (B) to make it possible for the child to return to his home. . .

(16) provides for the development of a case plan (as defined in section 475(1) for each child receiving foster care maintenance payments under the state plan and provides for a case review system which meets the requirements described in section 475(5)(B) with respect to each such child. (94 STAT 502, Sec. 471)

*Payments*

The adoption assistance program provided under P.L. 96-272 outlines requirements on the amount of payments, restrictions on payments, and children with special needs as:

(2) The amount of the adoption assistance payments shall be determined through agreement between the adoptive parents and the state or local agency administering the program under this section, which shall take into consideration the circumstances of the adopting parents and the needs of the child being adopted, and may be readjusted periodically, with the concurrence of the adopting parents (which may be specified in the adoption assistance agreement), depending upon changes in such circumstances. However, in no case may the amount of the adoption assistance payment exceed the foster care maintenance payment which would have been paid during the period if the child with respect to whom the adoption assistance payment is made had been in a foster family home.

(3) Notwithstanding the preceding paragraph, (A) no payment may be made to parents with respect to any child who has attained the age of eighteen (or, where the state determines that the child has a mental or physical handicap which warrants the continuation of assistance, the age of twenty-one), and (B) no payment may be made to parents with respect to any child if the state determines that the parents are no longer legally responsible for the support of the child or if the state determines that the child is no longer receiving any support from such parents. Parents who have been receiving adoption assistance payments under this section shall keep the state or local agency administering the program under this section informed of circumstances which would, pursuant to this subsection, make them ineligible for such assistance payments, or eligible for assistance payments in a different amount.

(4) For purposes of this part, individuals with whom a child (who has been determined by the state, pursuant to subsection C, to be a child with special needs) is placed for adoption, pursuant to an interlocutory decree, shall be eligible for adoption assistance payments under this subsection, during the period of the placement, on the same terms and subject to the same conditions as if such individuals had adopted such child.

(b) For purposes of title XIX and XX, any child with respect to whom adoption assistance payments are made under this section shall be deemed to be a dependent child as defined in section 406 and shall be deemed to be a recipient of aid to families with dependent children under part A of this title.

(c) For purposes of this section, a child shall not be considered a child with special needs unless—

(1) the state has determined that the child cannot or should not be returned to the home of his parents; and

(2) the state had first determined (A) that there exists with respect to the child a specific factor or condition (such as his ethnic background, age, or membership in a minority or sibling group, or the presence of factors such as medical conditions or physical, mental, or emotional handicaps) because of which it is reasonable to conclude that such child cannot be placed with adoptive parents without providing adoption assistance, and (B) that, except where it would be against the best interests of the child because of such factors as the existence of significant emotional ties with prospective adoptive parents while in the care of such parents as a foster child, a reasonable, but successful, effort has been made to place the child with appropriate adoptive parents without providing adoption assistance under this section. (94 STAT 505, Sec. 473)

## Child Welfare Services

The detailed description of child welfare services in P.L. 96-272 means:

Public social services which are directed toward the accomplishment of the following purposes: (A) protecting and promoting the welfare of all children, including handicapped, homeless, dependent, or neglected children; (B) preventing or remedying, or assisting in the solution of problems which may result in the neglect, abuse, exploitation, or delinquency of children; (C) preventing the unnecessary separation of children from their families by identifying family problems, assisting families in resolving their problems, and preventing breakup of family where the prevention of child removal is desirable and possible; (D) restoring to their families children who have been removed, by the provision of services to the child and the families; (E) placing children in suitable adoptive homes, in cases where restoration to the biological family is not possible or appropriate; and (F) assuring adequate care of children away from their homes, in cases where the child cannot be returned home or cannot be placed for adoption. (94 STAT 519, Sec. 425 [a][1])

## Other Provisions

Other general provisions of P.L. 96-272 pertaining to all children include federal payments for dependent children voluntarily placed in foster care, child welfare services, social care services, matching for child day-care expenditures, emergency shelter, shelter allowances, and incentives for states to collect child-support obligations.

## Child Abuse Prevention and Treatment Act of 1974

The Child Abuse Prevention and Treatment Act of 1974 (P.L. 93-247) defines child abuse and neglect as:

The physical or mental injury, sexual abuse, negligent treatment, or maltreatment of a child under the age of eighteen by a person who is responsible for the child's welfare under circumstances which indicate that the child's health or welfare is harmed or threatened thereby. (P.L. 93-247, Sec. 3)

## State Plan

In order for states to receive assistance under P.L. 93-247, such states shall:

(A) have in effect a state child abuse and neglect law which shall include provisions for immunity for persons reporting state or local law, arising out of such reporting;

(B) provide for the reporting of known and suspected instances of child abuse and neglect;

(C) provide that upon receipt of a report of known or suspected instances of child abuse or neglect an investigation shall be initiated promptly to substantiate the accuracy of the report and, upon a finding of abuse or neglect, immediate steps shall be taken to protect the health and welfare of the abused or neglected child, as well as that of any other child under the same care who may be in danger of abuse or neglect;

(D) demonstrate that there are in effect throughout the state, in connection with the enforcement of child abuse and neglect laws and with the reporting of suspected instances of child abuse and neglect, such administrative procedures, such personnel trained in child abuse and neglect prevention and treatment, such training procedures, such institutional and other facilities (public and private), and such related multidisciplinary programs and services as may be necessary or appropriate to assure that the state will deal effectively with child abuse and neglect cases in the state;

(E) provide for methods to preserve the confidentiality of all records in order to protect the rights of the child, his parents or guardians;

(F) provide for the cooperation of law enforcement officials, courts of competent jurisdiction, and appropriate state agencies providing human services;

(G) provide that in every case involving an abused or neglected child which results in a judicial proceeding a guardian ad litem shall be appointed to represent the child in such proceedings;

(H) provide that the aggregate of support for programs or projects related to child abuse and neglect assisted by state funds shall not be reduced below the level provided during fiscal year 1973, and set forth policies and procedures designed to assure that federal funds made available under this act for any fiscal year will be so used as to supplement and, to the extent practical, increase the level of state funds which would, in the absence of federal funds, be available for such programs and projects;

(I) provide for dissemination of information to the general public with respect to the problem of child abuse and neglect and the facilities and prevention and treatment methods available to combat instances of child abuse and neglect; and

(J) to the extent feasible, insure that parental organizations combating child abuse and neglect receive preferential treatment. (P.L. 93-247, Sec. 4)

## National Housing Act of 1976

The National Housing Act makes provisions for loans for housing and related facilities for elderly or handicapped families. Also provided are rent supplement payments and handicapped family units and rental preference or priority. (12 U.S.C.S. § 1701[q], [s], and [v])

## Omnibus Budget Reconciliation Act of 1981

The Omnibus Budget Reconciliation Act of 1981 (P.L. 97-35) permits states to offer home and community-based services that one might need to avoid being placed in an institution.

*Provisions*

The regulations:

(1) Provide that certain facilities must meet standards, including those established under section 1618(e) of the Social Security Act, if waiver services are to be provided in the facilities, (2) revise the equation that states must use to determine the cost-effectiveness of their waiver programs, (3) clarify that these services are available, at a state's option, to both medically needy individuals and categorically needy individuals, (4) provide that all recipients who are eligible under a special income level will have their post-eligibility income treated in a comparable manner, (5) revise some aspects of the assurances and the documentaion that states must provide in their waiver requests, (6) revise the effective date of an approved wavier, (7) established a federal financial participation (FFP) limit for expenditures for home and community-based services, and (8) specify the hearings procedures that apply to waiver terminations. (Federal Register, Vol. 50, No. 49, p. 10013)

*Home Care*

Home or community-based services furnished under a waiver must be health-oriented and not vocational in nature. The services may consist of:

(a) Case management services;
(b) Homemaker services;
(c) Home health aide services;
(d) Personal care services;
(e) Adult day health services;
(f) Habilitation services;
(g) Respite care services;
(h) Other services requested by the Medicaid agency approved by HCFA as cost-effective. (Federal Register, Vol. 50, No. 49, p. 10026)

## EDUCATIONAL PROVISIONS

Because of evidence provided by a variety of advocacy groups and related litigation, Congress recognized the need to outline the educational provisions for handicapped children.

## Education for All Handicapped Children Act of 1975

The Education for All Handicapped Children Act of 1975 (P.L. 94-142) assures a free appropriate public education to handicapped children emphasizing special education and related services designed to meet their unique needs as documented in an individualized education program.

### *Definitions*

The following terms are defined for clarity:

(16) The term "special education" means specially designed instruction, at no cost to parents or guardians, to meet the unique needs of a handicapped child, including classroom instruction, instruction in physical education, home instruction, and instruction in hospitals and institutions.

(17) The term "related services" means transportation, and such developmental, corrective, and other supportive services (including speech pathology and audiology, psychological services, physical and occupational therapy, recreation, and medical and counseling services, except that such medical services shall be for diagnostic and evaluation purposes only) as may be required to assist a handicapped child to benefit from special education, and includes the early identification and assessment of handicapping conditions in children.

(18) The term "free appropriate public education" means special education and related services which (A) have been provided at public expense, under public supervision and direction, and without charge, (B) meet the standards of the state educational agency, (C) include an appropriate preschool, elementary, or secondary school education in the state involved, and (D) are provided in conformity with the individualized education program required under section 614(a) (5).

(19) The term "individualized education program" means a written statement for each handicapped child developed in any meeting by a representative of the local educational agency or an intermediate educational unit who shall be qualified to provide, or supervise the provision of, specially designed instruction to meet the unique needs of handicapped children, the teacher, the parents or guardian of such child, and, whenever appropriate, such child, which statement shall include (A) a statement of the present levels

of educational performance of such child, (B) a statement of annual goals, including short-term instructional objectives, (C) a statement of the specific educational services to be provided to such child, and the extent to which such child will be able to participate in regular educational programs, (D) the projected date for initiation and anticipated duration of such services, and (E) appropriate objective criteria and evaluation procedures and schedules for determining, on at least an annual basis, whether instructional objectives are being achieved. (20 U.S.C. 1401, Sec. 4)

The procedural safeguards under P.L. 94-142 provide the parents of a handicapped child the opportunity to review all records, to obtain independent evaluations, to protect the rights of the child when parents are unavailable, outlines procedures for written notices to meetings and an option for formal hearings. (20 U.S.C. 1415)

## Vocational Education Amendments

The Vocational Education Amendments of 1975 (P.L. 94-482) established priority allotments of state funds for vocational education programs designed for special needs youth. Special needs learners are the handicapped and disadvantaged. A priority allotment of 10 percentum was reserved for handicapped persons. (20 U.S.C.S. § 2310)

## REHABILITATION PROVISIONS

### Rehabilitation Act of 1973

The Rehabilitation Act of 1973 (P.L. 93-112) provides a statutory basis for the Rehabilitation Services Administration and authorizes program development in a number of ways.

### *Specific Programs*

The specific programs authorized by P.L. 93-112 are to:

(1) develop and implement comprehensive and continuing state plans for meeting the current and future needs for providing vocational rehabilitation services to handicapped individuals and to provide such services for the benefit of such individual, serving first those with the most severe handicaps, so that they may prepare for and engage in gainful employment;

(2) evaluate the rehabilitation potential of handicapped individuals;

(3) conduct a study to develop methods of providing rehabilitation services to meet the current and future needs of handicapped individuals for whom a vocational goal is not possible or feasible so that they may improve their ability to live with greater independence and self-sufficiency;

(4) assist in the construction and improvement of rehabilitation facilities;

(5) develop new and innovative methods of applying the most advanced medical technology, scientific achievement, and psychological and social knowledge to solve rehabilitation problems and develop new and innovative methods of providing rehabilitation services to handicapped individuals through research, special projects, and demonstrations;

(6) initiate and expand services to groups of handicapped individuals (including those who are homebound or institutionalized) who have been underserved in the past;

(7) conduct various studies and experiments to focus on long neglected problem areas;

(8) promote and expand employment opportunities in the public and private sectors for handicapped individuals and to place such individuals in employment;

(9) establish client assistance pilot projects;

(10) provide assistance for the purpose of increasing the number of rehabilitation personnel and increasing their skills through training; and

(11) evaluate existing approaches to architectural and transportation barriers confronting handicapped individuals, develop new such approaches, enforce statutory and regulatory standards and requirements regarding barrier-free construction of public facilities and study and develop solutions to existing architectural and transportation barriers impeding handicapped individuals. (29 U.S.C.S. 701, § 2)

## Severe Handicapping Conditions

For purposes of this act, the term "severe handicap" means:
The disability which requires multiple services over an extended period of time and results from amputation, blindness, cancer, cerebral palsy, cystic fibrosis, deafness, heart disease, hemiplegia, mental retardation, mental illness, multiple sclerosis, muscular dystrophy, neurological disorders (including stroke and epilepsy),

paraplegia, quadriplegia and other spinal cord conditions, renal failure, and any other disability specified by the secretary in regulations he shall prescribe. (29 U.S.C.S. 701 § 7 [12])

## Services Provided

The scope of vocational rehabilitation services provided under P.L. 93-112 are those goods and services deemed appropriate to make a handicapped individual employable, including:

(1) evaluation of rehabilitation potential, including diagnostic and related services, incidental to the determination of eligibility for, and the nature and scope of, services to be provided, including, where appropriate, examination by a physician skilled in the diagnosis and treatment of emotional disorders, or by a licensed psychologist in accordance with state laws and regulations, or both;

(2) counseling, guidance, referral, and placement services for handicapped individuals, including follow-up, follow-along, and other post-employment services necessary to assist such individuals to maintain their employment and services designed to help handicapped individuals secure needed services from other agencies, where such services are not available under this act;

(3) vocational and other training services for handicapped individuals, which shall include personal and vocational adjustment, books, and other training materials, and services to the families of such individuals as are necessary to the adjustment or rehabilitation of such individuals: *Provided,* that no training services in institutions of higher education shall be paid for with funds under this title unless maximum efforts have been made to secure grant assistance, in whole or in part, from other sources to pay for such training;

(4) physical and mental restoration sevices, including, but not limited to, (A) corrective surgery or therapeutic treatment necessary to correct or substantially modify a physical or mental condition which is stable or slowly progressive and constitutes a substantial handicap to employment, but is of such nature that such correction or modification may reasonably be expected to eliminate or substantially reduce the handicap within a reasonable length of time, (B) necessary hospitalization in connection with surgery or treatment, (C) prosthetic and orthotic devices, (D) eyeglasses and visual services as prescribed by a physician skilled in the diseases of the eye or by an optometrist, whichever the individual may select, (E) special services (including transplantation and dialysis), artifi-

cial kidneys, and supplies necessary for the treatment of individuals suffering from end-stage renal disease, and (F) diagnosis and treatment for mental and emotional disorders by a physician or licensed psychologist in accordance with state licensure laws;

(5) maintenance, not exceeding the estimated cost of subsistence, during rehabilitation;

(6) interpreter services for deaf individuals, and reader services for those individuals determined to be blind after an examination by a physician skilled in the diseases of the eye or by an optometrist, whichever the individual may select;

(7) recruitment and training services for handicapped individuals to provide them with new employment opportunities in the fields of rehabilitation, health, welfare, public safety, and law enforcement, and other appropriate service employment;

(8) rehabilitation teaching services and orientation and mobility services for the blind;

(9) occupational licenses, tools, equipment, and initial stocks and supplies;

(10) transportation in connection with the rendering of any vocational rehabilitation services; and

(11) telecommunications, sensory, and other technological aids and devices. (29 U.S.C.S. § 723 [a])

It is through this act that handicapped individuals are guaranteed an equal opportunity to training, employment, and access to public transportation and public buildings constructed since 1975.

## Rehabilitation Amendments of 1984

The Rehabilitation Amendments of 1984 (P.L. 98-221) provides (1) in making a determination of ineligibility that emphasis be placed on the determination and achievement of a vocational goal, (2) if the individual is determined not capable of obtaining the stated goal, that the decision be made in full consultation with the individual and the plan be amended certifying the client was not capable of achieving stated goal, and (3) the written amendment should be reviewed annually. (29 U.S.C.S. § 722 [c])

## SEQUESTRATION

Sequestration is a provision for automatic cutbacks in spending. This provision was invoked to reduce the federal budget deficit.

## Gramm-Rudman Federal Deficit Reduction Amendment of 1985

The Gramm-Rudman Federal Deficit Reduction Amendment of 1985 was passed December 11, 1985, and requires a balanced budget by Fiscal Year 1991. Under automatic reductions, programs serving individuals with developmental disabilities (such as Medicaid, SSI, and Social Security) will be protected. Other vital programs subject to cuts in funding include special education, vocational rehabilitation, maternal and child health, and developmental disabilities. (*Arc. GAO*, 12/13/85)

One consequence which is likely is that programs, state plans, and rights for the developmentally disabled will have been established, but funding cuts and inflation will weaken their effectiveness. If substantial budget cuts are made, monitoring and enforcement of statutes will be significantly lessened. Unfortunately, without the threat of court order or enforcement of statutes, society typically does not serve its developmentally disabled members.

## SUMMARY

A brief overview of the rights and services provided the developmentally disabled has been presented for the areas of social, educational, and rehabilitation needs. During the last decade, significant gains have been made to assure that the developmentally disabled have an equal opportunity to basic life needs and services.

The bottom line on service delivery is contingent on professional commitment and funding. Funding cuts from the federal level appear to be a reality. If the current rate of care provided the developmentally disabled is to continue, individual states must fund programs at an increased level. Social workers should be professionally committed to advocate individual rights and services to their clientele.

## NOTES

1. Chapter 3 was written by Ernest E. Singletary, Ed.D., Associate Professor, Department of Special Education, University of Alabama at Birmingham.

# Part II

# INTRODUCTION

TWENTY-THREE syndromes are selected for discussion in Part
II. The format for presenting each syndrome includes: (1) a brief
introduction to the syndromes, (2) the etiology, (3) diagnostic procedures, (4) signs and symptoms, (5) mental retardation levels, (6) treatment concerns, and (7) case histories. Mental retardation is a prominent
feature with most of the syndromes described but is associated only occasionally with some of the other disorders such as spina bifida, Turner
syndrome, Klinefelter syndrome, and hydrocephalus. The syndromes,
all prenatal in origin, are organized for presentation according to
etiology. Disorders with a genetic etiology are discussed in Chapters
Four, Five, and Six. Included are examples of chromosomal, single
gene, and multifactorial (polygenic) disorders. Chapter Seven reviews
various disorders of unknown etiology in addition to one endocrine disorder and one disorder caused by an infection (cytomegalic inclusion
disease). All cases presented in these chapters were evaluated at the
Sparks Center for Developmental and Learning Disorders, University
of Alabama at Birmingham.

## Chapter Four

# CHROMOSOMAL DISORDERS

E ACH CELL (except reproductive cells) in a normal human being contains 23 matched pairs of chromosomes: 22 autosomes and one sex (X) chromosome inherited from the mother, and 22 autosomes and one sex (X or Y) chromosome inherited from the father. A normal male has a 46, XY karyotype (the pictorial arrangement of matched pairs of chromosomes), and a normal female has a 46, XX karyotype. Sometimes, an individual will not have the normal number of 46 chromosomes, or defects will exist in the structure of a chromosome. These errors may involve the autosomes (the first 22 matched pairs of chromosomes are called the autosomes) or the sex chromosomes (X or Y). The error occurs during cell division (nondisjunction), which takes place during the final phases of the formation of the ovum or sperm prior to or during fertilization. Chromosome errors cause multiple birth defects, but a very high percentage of conceptions with a chromosomal abnormality terminates in spontaneous abortion. About 0.5–1 percent of all newborns have birth defects associated with chromosome abnormalities. This chapter reviews a few syndromes caused by chromosomal errors, including Down syndrome, an autosomal abnormality, and two sex chromosome disorders, Turner and Klinefelter syndromes. Additionally, fragile X syndrome is discussed.

### AUTOSOMAL ABNORMALITIES

Most often, a chromosome error is numerial (i.e. each cell contains an incorrect number of chromosomes). Down syndrome (trisomy 21), one of the more commonly known disorders associated with mental retardation, is generally the result of a chromosome numerical error. Individuals with the disorder have an extra chromosome on the 21st pair;

thus, each cell in the body contains 47 instead of 46 chromosomes. Down syndrome occurs about 1/800 births, whereas Edward syndrome (trisomy 18) occurs about 1/8,000 births and Patau syndrome (trisomy 13) occurs about 1/20,000 births (Summitt, 1978).

The breakage of segments of a chromosome may result in:

A *translocation* (a fragment of one chromosome breaks off and becomes attached to another chromosome);
A *deletion* (the loss of one or more chromosome segments);
A *duplication* (a double number of identical genes appears on a single chromosome);
An *inversion* (a two-point break on a chromosome, with segments becoming reattached in reverse order). (Levine, 1978, p. 10)

A person may carry a balanced translocation and be phenotypically (external appearance) normal, but his/her offspring will be at increased risk of having an unbalanced translocation and birth defects. About 3 percent of individuals with Down syndrome have a normal number of 46 chromosomes, but extra material from the 21st pair may be attached to another chromosome, usually number 14. When this occurs, one parent carries the 14/21 balanced translocation. A carrier father has about a 2–5 percent risk of having a child with Down syndrome of this type; the risk for a carrier mother is about 10–15 percent. Translocation Down syndrome is clinically similar to other Down cases but is not necessarily related to maternal age.

When chromosomes have deletions or duplications, the affected person usually has multiple and severe abnormalities. The cat cry (cri du chat) syndrome is an example of a deletion in a number 5 chromosome. The affected infant is characterized by a cry similar to that of a cat. Such infants also are mentally retarded and have a number of abnormal clinical features.

Many birth defects are associated with the autosomal disorders. Perhaps mental retardation is the most consistent feature found among all these disorders. However, many other clinical abnormalities are found with these disorders, including short stature, seizures, eye abnormalities, ear abnormalities, dental problems, cardiac defects, renal anomalies, and orthopedic problems, as well as many other abnormal craniofacial features.

## Down Syndrome (Trisomy 21)

Down syndrome has characteristic features that are easily recognized. The incidence of Down syndrome is reported to vary from approximately one in 600 to one in 800 births. In the early childbearing years, the incidence is about one in 2,000 births; for mothers more than 40 years of age, it rises to about 45 in 1,000. Investigators have known for some time that the risk of having a child with this syndrome increases with advancing maternal age, but the reason for this has not been discovered. (Batshaw & Perret, 1981; Gorlin, Pindborg, & Cohen, 1976; Richmond, Tarjan, & Mendelsohn, 1976)

## Etiology

Trisomy 21, which accounts for about 94 percent of all Down syndrome cases, is caused by a genetic defect and is thought to occur when either the egg or the sperm contributes an extra chromosome at conception. At this point the cause of the improper cell division leading to Down syndrome is unknown, but some authorities believe that such factors as viral infections, hormonal abnormalities, exposure to radiation, drugs, or a genetic predisposition may be involved in the process of nondisjunction (failure of the chromosomes to separate properly). As a result of the failure of the No. 21 pair to separate, an additional chromosome is present in the cells of the human body. This extra 21st chromosome, for some unknown reason, produces the mental and physical characteristics of Down syndrome.

## Diagnosis

Clinical suspicion of Down syndrome is confirmed commonly through chromosome studies performed at a genetics laboratory.

Prenatal diagnosis of Down syndrome is made through a process called amniocentesis which comprises withdrawal of small amounts of fluid surrounding the fetus from the amniotic sac. Examination of the cultured cells from this fluid shows whether or not the mother is carrying a baby with abnormal chromosomes. Amniocentesis, which is performed at about the sixteenth week of gestation, frequently is advised for "high-risk" expectant mothers (i.e. those past the age of 35 and those who have already given birth to a child with Down syndrome). Once parents have a child with Down syndrome, regardless of maternal age, there is an increased risk of one in 100 of having another baby with the disorder in future pregnancies. If, however, the child has the translocation type of Down syndrome, which occurs with less frequency, the risk increases and the disorder may be carried by a normal-appearing parent or sibling.

## Signs and Symptoms

More than 65 symptoms of Down syndrome have been listed, but no single individual has them all. Some of the more common features of

Down syndrome include: mental retardation; short stature; upward eye slant with epicanthal folds; Brushfield spots (white spots around the iris); flat occiput (back of head); flat nose; high arched palate; protruding, deeply fissured tongue; poorly developed and distributed teeth; small, low-set ears; hyperflexibility of joints; short, broad fingers; hypotonia (weak muscle tone); and a simian crease in the palm of the hands.

### Mental Retardation

The range of mental retardation with Down syndrome extends from severe to near normal.

### Treatment Concerns

With Down syndrome, the diagnosis usually is evident at birth. This results in parents being given distressing information at a time when emotions and expectations are high. Nevertheless, according to some reports parents prefer to be told of the diagnosis within the first week (Gayton & Walker, 1974). Both parents should be present when the diagnosis is discussed, and a physician who is familiar with the family should present the information. Also, genetic counseling should be an essential part of the treatment plan. Specialized medical and surgical treatment in infancy may be required for such problems as congenital heart disease and duodenal atresia (congenital closure of a portion of the duodenum). Other treatment requirements may include: (1) audiology for hearing impairments subsequent to upper-respiratory infections; (2) speech therapy for language delays and articulation problems; (3) nutritional services for weight control; (4) sex education; (5) special education; (6) supervised versus independent living; (7) structured employment; (8) dental care (many patients develop periodontal disease during the adult years); and (9) visual care for problems such as farsightedness, nearsightedness, and squinting (strabismus).

### Case Study

Gina, a 2½-year-old female with Down syndrome, was seen at the Sparks Center for interdisciplinary evaluations. She was the product of an uneventful pregnancy and a 16-hour delivery with low forceps assist. Birthweight was 6 pounds, 9 ounces. Features consistent with Down syndrome, as well as a bowel obstruction, possibly Hirschsprung disease, were noted at birth. Genetic studies confirmed the diagnosis of Down syndrome. Hirschsprung disease was diagnosed at 3 months of age, with a subsequent colostomy being performed. She had been hospitalized numerous times for gastroenteritis and dehydration. The mother reported that diarrhea was a problem due to Gina's shortened intestine. She had several episodes of otitis media (ear infection) and tubes were placed in both ears.

Gina resided with both of her natural parents and a 2-year-old brother in a rural area of east Tennessee. Gina's father, age 36, was an unemployed construction worker. The mother, age 35, was a school teacher. The maternal grandmother, it was reported, provided an extreme amount of help to Gina's parents. In addition to helping with the children, she had provided financial assistance. Both parents were unprepared, as most people would be, for the diagnosis and were only vaguely familiar with the disorder. The mother was completely devastated when told of the diagnosis and almost required hospitalization. She stayed depressed for weeks at a time and had asked herself many times "why me." Both parents expressed the belief that it was "God's will" for them as "special people" to have a "special child."

After being told about a certain type of therapy called "cell therapy," the mother began to investigate these procedures and later Gina did receive this type of therapy in another state. According to the parents, the therapy had not brought about the results for which they had hoped. Yet, they were afraid to discontinue the therapy because of the chance that it might "do some good." The cost of treatment was more than the family could afford and several family members had made financial contributions towards this therapy.

The Sparks Center recommended more traditional approaches to care. These included preschool programs, speech and language therapy, self-help training, and supportive counseling for the parents.

## SEX CHROMOSOMAL ABNORMALITIES

Abnormal combinations of sex chromosomes appear to cause less damage than do errors in the other chromosomes (autosomes). The sex chromosome abnormalities are not heritable, except in rare translocations, and the recurrence risk in the affected individual's family is extremely small (Schimke, 1978).

Turner syndrome (XO syndrome) is an example of a sex chromosome abnormality found in families. Individuals with the disorder have one X chromosome. The most consistent features of the disorder are small stature and failure of sexual maturation.

Klinefelter syndrome is a sex chromosome abnormality affecting males who have a 47,XXY sex chromosome complement. Other variants of Klinefelter syndrome exist; there can be further increases in the number of X chromosomes (i.e. an XXXY complement). Mental retardation, when present in the XXXY male, usually is more severe than when found in the XXY male.

Females with an extra X (47,XXX) and males with an extra Y (47,XYY) are examples of other chromosome abnormalities. With the XXX females, distinct physical characteristics are not always evident, although the distribution of their IQ scores tends to fall in the mental retardation category. The XYY males usually are more than six feet tall, and they may have seizures, acne, and skeletal abnormalities. Males with the disorder allegedly exhibit sociopathic behavior, but research (primarily in penal institutions) has not confirmed conclusively any link between the XYY syndrome and criminal behavior.

## Klinefelter Syndrome

Klinefelter syndrome, a sex chromosomal abnormality, affects only males. The disorder is not usually apparent until the teenage years when there is a delay in secondary sexual development. Estimates indicate that one in every 1,000 males is born with the disorder. (Apgar & Beck, 1974; Cunningham, 1970; Opitz, 1973)

### Etiology

One or more extra (X) chromosomes are present in the affected male.

### Diagnosis

The diagnosis is made by cytogenetic studies.

### Signs and Symptoms

The clinical symptoms are: small testes; a tall slender build or obesity; female-like breasts (gynecomastia); occasionally visual problems; and occasionally mental retardation or slow learning ability. Behavioral or anti-social tendencies are present in some individuals and may vary from mild to severe.

## *Mental Retardation*

The level of mental retardation, if present, is usually in the mild range.

## *Treatment Concerns*

Mental retardation, learning difficulties, personality problems, and the physical stigmata of the disorder present the main treatment considerations. Enlarged breasts can be eliminated by surgery; sexual traits can be stimulated with testosterone therapy; and learning problems will require special education or remedial programs. The personality problems may be more difficult to treat, but if the patient is amenable to medical or surgical treatment, improvement in the body image may result in improvements with behavior. Genetic counseling is indicted for both parents and the patient. Although it is not likely that affected males will ever father a child, they need to understand the disorder before they can adjust to the diagnosis.

## *Case Study*

Danny, age 14, was referred to the Sparks Center for evaluation of learning difficulties and psychosocial problems associated with Klinefelter syndrome. His natural mother was divorced from both the biological father and his adoptive stepfather. There were two other siblings — a sister, age 17, and a brother, age 15. The mother was unemployed and the family received Medicaid and ADC.

Danny had completed the seventh grade at a local school where he attended a learning disability resource class. He had repeated one other year of school. The teachers reported that he participated poorly in class, sucked his thumb, and had no involvement with peers, which, of course, made him feel left out. The mother reported that he did have a few friends but tended to argue with them often. Danny had a very quick temper which became evident while he was in the fourth grade when he threatened to kill a teacher. He was expelled from school and sent to a local psychiatric facility for the remainder of the year. The family participated in therapy sessions, but the mother reported that it only caused more confusion.

Danny returned to his regular school, and after several difficult years he was again referred for psychiatric treatment. He now had reached the early adolescent years. It was noted that Danny was very conscious of his height and weight, both of which were above the 75th percentile. He also was embarrassed to change clothes for PE classes, so he settled for an "F" in this class. Because of his unusual size, behavioral problems and enlarged breasts, genetic studies were requested and these confirmed the suspected diagnosis of Klinefelter syndrome. Because the teachers were unaware of the physical and emotional problems resulting from this syndrome, they did not take this into account in his refusal to cooperate. Also, a referral for testosterone therapy was made to an adolescent clinic at the local university medical center, but this was discouraged due to the fact that it made him more aggressive than he previously had been.

At the Sparks Center, the physician who examined Danny found no significant medical problems other than those related to Klinefelter syndrome. Dentistry found rampant tooth decay, and he faced the likelihood of losing all of his teeth in the near future if treatment were not started soon. His academic scores placed him at the second-grade level in math, fourth-grade level in reading, and first-grade level in general information. During the evaluations at Sparks Center, Danny was totally uncooperative. Staff consensus was that Danny needed some type of counseling where the mother also could be involved. Someone in a professional capacity needed to tell the mother in a straightforward manner that if she did not develop a more age-appropriate attitude toward her son and did not begin consistently to require responsible behavior from him, his basic genetic medical problem was going to be immeasurably harder to manage.

### Turner Syndrome (XO Syndrome)

Turner syndrome is a disorder in which the female has only one X chromosome, resulting in faulty sexual development (gonadal dysgenesis), occasionally mental retardation, and various other physical anomalies. Turner syndrome occurs about one in every 3,000 newborns. (Blackman, 1983; Menkes, 1985; Smith, 1982; Schimke, 1978)

#### *Etiology*

The disorder is caused by a chromosomal aberration. Females with the disorder have the usual 44 autosomes, but only one X chromosome.

#### *Diagnosis*

The diagnosis is made through chromosomal studies.

## Signs and Symptoms

The primary features of this disorder include: webbed neck; short stature; infantile sexual development; atypical facies; puffiness of the hands and feet; underdeveloped fingernails and toenails (hypoplastic); small, widely spaced nipples, and anomalies of the extremities. Hearing or vision problems may be present, as well as kidney abnormalities.

## Mental Retardation

Mental retardation is not a common feature of Turner syndrome, although there are cases with mild mental retardation. The problem with the disorder, however, is in the area of spatial perception; this produces a discrepancy on IQ tests between verbal ability and performance level. This cognitive deficit has led some researchers to consider the possibility that X chromosome genes might be involved in various visual-spatial abilities.

## Treatment Concerns

Special remedial work in school probably will be required because of hearing or cognitive problems. Visual difficulties also may need attention so as not to complicate the educational planning. Personal counseling dealing with personality adjustment and poor self-concept may be a factor to consider. Otherwise, medical care will depend on the health status of the individual, but more than likely health problems needing attention will involve the heart or kidneys.

## Case Study

At age 6, Leslie was seen by an interdisciplinary team at the Sparks Center to evaluate her developmental delays associated with Turner syndrome. Initial concerns were her small size (height and weight were below the 5th percentile), poor appetite, delayed speech, and a tendency to contract infections. She had a history of heart and kidney problems that had required frequent hospitalizations. Prenatal history revealed that there were no prenatal or major problems at birth. However, as an infant, Leslie appeared quite swollen and was transferred to the university's high-risk nursery for five weeks. Again, she was hospitalized at 7 weeks with respiratory distress. Since that time, she had been admitted to the hospital on several occasions with congestive heart failure and seizures.

At the Sparks Center, she was found to be mildly retarded. She also had a severe articulation problem and, in general, had developmental delays in all areas, including the social, self-help, academic, communication, and physical. In view of these delays, her attendance at special classes was necessary.

Leslie was the youngest of three children from a low-income family. Two older boys had marked speech delays and were attending special education classes. The mother was a housewife and the father was a laborer for a landscaping firm; however, according to the mother, they rarely saw the father's income, as he spent it "drinking and running around." The couple had severe, longstanding marital problems and they had separated on at least two occasions. The father had shown no more than a passing interest in Leslie's problems. The social worker believed that the mother also did not realize the implications of all of Leslie's problems. She seemed to see the difficulties in purely medical terms and really did not seem to understand or be able to admit to herself that slow mental development was a possible factor in the case.

About one year after the initial evaluation, the father came in to the center to report that the mother had been hospitalized with a "heart attack and a tumor on her thyroid." She also had diabetes and would require hospitalization over an extended period of time. The social worker got the impression that Leslie's father seemed to be demonstrating more interest in her welfare, and perhaps his wife's acute illness might have overshadowed some of the existing marital problems. Leslie seemed more alert and less dependent. She was attending special classes and also was receiving speech therapy.

## X-LINKED MENTAL RETARDATION

The X-linked type of mental retardation came to be recognized by observing families in which only males were affected and by noting the known higher incidence of mental retardation in males. The fragile X syndrome is a type of X-linked mental retardation and is thought to be a fairly common chromosomal cause of mental retardation in males. Because the condition covers a large range of physical findings, identification by external appearance may be difficult. The following discussion of the fragile X syndrome and the case history provide a description of a sub-category of X-linked mental retardation.

## Fragile X Syndrome

Fragile X syndrome is an inherited disorder primarily affecting males who are typically developmentally delayed with mild to moderate mental retardation. Next to Down syndrome, it is thought to be the most common chromosomal cause of mental retardation in males. The disorder is estimated to affect one in every 1,000 to 2,000 live-born males. (Hagerman, 1984; Hagerman & McBogg, 1983; Hagerman et al., 1983; Harvey, Judge & Wiener, 1977; Howard-Peebles & Finley, 1983; Sutherland & Ashforth, 1979)

### Etiology

Genetic studies from affected individuals show that the distal end of the X chromosome appears to be connected to the rest of the chromosome by a thin broken region. The disorder follows the X-linked recessive pattern of inheritance.

### Diagnosis

The disorder should be suspected when an individual in question shows a family history of mental retardation limited to males, especially if the individual has certain clinical features (e.g. large ears, large testicles, and mental retardation). The diagnosis is made by chromosomal studies. The fragile X syndrome can be detected prenatally through analysis of the amniotic fluid, but the results are not accurate in all cases.

### Signs and Symptoms

With variation from patient to patient, manifestations of the disorder are: a large head; mid-facial defective development (hypoplasia); prominent forehead; a long, narrow face; prominent chin; high arched palate; and enlarged ears. Enlarged testicles (macro-orchidism) commonly are associated with the disorder and, if present, usually are found among postpubertal affected males, though the characteristic has been found in younger males. Hyperextensible finger joints or "double-jointedness" are found in some patients. Short stature has been observed, but this seems to be the exception rather than the rule. Speech and language dysfunctions are frequently found with the fragile X patient, including echolalia, perseveration, dysfluency, and articulation deficits. Behavioral problems sometimes are associated with the disorder, including autistic-like behavior, self-abusive behavior, hyperactivity, hand flapping, self-isolation, need for order, and, in general, bizarre behaviors. Some affected males will not show any particular external characteristics.

Approximately 50 percent of the carrier females, referred to as heterozygous fragile X females, will be mildly retarded or have learning disabilities. Some females will manifest milder forms of the physical anomalies (e.g. prominent ears, elongated facies, high foreheads, high arched palates, and hyperextensible finger joints).

### Mental Retardation

The level of mental retardation is mild to moderate.

### Treatment Concerns

The importance of genetic counseling is clearly evident in view of the manner in which the disorder is transmitted and the effects it has on immediate and extended family members. The disorder is X-linked and as such is passed from generation to generation, primarily affecting males, and, to some extent, a high percentage of carrier females. In families where the disorder has been identified, a family history or pedigree can help identify female members who might need heterozygote screening to determine if they carry the abnormal genetic materials for fragile X. A negative cytogenetic analysis from a female in such a family does not rule out the risk of her being a carrier and having affected children. Each child of a carrier mother, regardless of sex, has a fifty-fifty chance of inheriting the genetic material for fragile X.

The genetic counseling process should include risk factors and information about the nature of the disorder, the prognosis, and the possible consequences of the disorder in relation to family life. It is important to emphasize that some of the mothers of fragile X males are themselves "mentally slow" and may not understand complicated genetic information. Consequently, extended counseling and support, utilizing other family members in the counseling process, is essential.

The treatment plan will involve special education; therapy for possible speech problems; therapy for those with severe motor problems, especially where sensorimotor integration is a problem; nutritional counseling when obesity occurs; and therapy for possible emotional dysfunctioning. Excessive anxiety and occasional behavioral problems are issues that sometimes need attention.

The fragile X syndrome offers a unique opportunity for the involvement of social work, not only in the diagnostic process where the family history may help ascertain the diagnosis, but in the treatment process as well. This role is especially important when in the general population the disorder is underdiagnosed, because screening for the fragile X site is not always feasible.

## Case Study

John, age 4 years and 9 months, came to the Sparks Center for evaluations at the insistence of an aunt who was concerned because of a history of mental retardation in the family. The father was very much opposed to the idea because he did not think there was anything wrong with John, or if there were, he would outgrow it. At the center, the diagnostic team suspected that John might have a disorder called fragile X, which was based on (1) his mental retardation, (2) his facial characteristics, and (3) a family history of mental retardation among males. Genetic studies did confirm the diagnosis of fragile X.

The social work evaluation found that John was an only child living with his natural parents in a housing project in a rural section of the state. His father, who earned a modest income, was in his early forties, a high school graduate, and employed at a meat-packing plant. John's mother, who also was in her early forties, had a third-grade education and was not employed outside the home; she had terminal cancer which was diagnosed about four years previously. Her pregnancy with John at age 37 was unexpected. Amniocentesis was attempted due to her advanced maternal age, but the tap was unsuccessful. The delivery was by C-section secondary to breech presentation. As described by the aunt, John had been overprotected since infancy. At almost age 5, he still was fearful of being separated from his mother and he did not like to be cared for by other people, including other family members.

The maternal family history was significant for mental retardation and a pedigree obtained during the social work interview indicated an X-linked pattern of inheritance on the maternal side (i.e. in this family females tended to have mentally retarded offspring). Also, John's physical features, according to the aunt, were similar to one maternal male first cousin and possibly a maternal uncle. The interview revealed that mental retardation in the maternal family included a great-uncle (institutionalized); two uncles (ages 34 and 31); two male first cousins (ages 12 and 9); and a son of a maternal great-aunt. A female first cousin, age 19, with two affected brothers received special education during her earlier school career. The aunt who reported this family history had no children, as her husband was unable to have children. In all the above cases the mental retardation was of undetermined etiology. As a result of the social work interview, one aunt, who was pregnant, was referred for genetic studies. She was found to be carrying a male; cytogenetic studies showed no fragile sites, and she appeared greatly relieved. The recommendation was made that another female cousin of John's, age 19, also be tested to determine carrier status.

John's mother died in the summer 1984. The social worker continued to work with this family on a number of issues such as acquiring SSI benefits, locating special education services, finding speech therapy and, in general, coordinating the case with other services. After the death of the mother, John remained for a short period of time with his father, who seemed to be taking on the responsibilities of caring for him much better than originally anticipated. John had trouble understanding the mother's death but nevertheless seemed to become more attached to the father. The two finally moved to another state where a maternal uncle and his wife had expressed an interest in caring for John.

## Chapter Five

# SINGLE GENE DISORDERS

S INGLE GENE disorders are classified as autosomal recessive, autosomal dominant, X-linked recessive, or X-linked dominant. Single
gene disorders affect about 1 percent of the population. Included for discussion in this chapter are four autosomal recessive disorders: phenylketonuria (PKU), argininosuccinic aciduria, galactosemia, and Seckel
syndrome. Under the dominant mode of inheritance, Apert syndrome,
tuberous sclerosis, and neurofibromatosis are discussed; under the X-
linked mode of inheritance, Coffin-Lowry and Hunter syndromes are
discussed.

## AUTOSOMAL RECESSIVE DISORDERS

An individual who has an autosomal recessive disorder must inherit
a matched pair of defective genes, one from each parent. The parents
are carriers, that is, they each carry the same defective gene for the disorder, but they do not manifest the disorder because each has an alternate or matched gene to counteract the harmful effects of the recessive
gene.

Each child born to parents who are carriers for an autosomal recessive disorder will inherit one of the following possible genotypes: (1) a 25
percent chance of inheriting two recessive genes and the disorder; (2) a
25 percent of inheriting two normal genes; and (3) a 50 percent chance
of inheriting one defective gene and becoming a carrier of the disorder.

Approximately 1,100 autosomal recessive disorders are confirmed or
suspected to date. Some disorders considered to be autosomal recessive
and involving mental retardation are Hurler syndrome, Wilson disease,
hereditary microcephaly, and Sanfilippo syndrome.

## Phenylketonuria

Phenylketonuria (PKU) is an inherited metabolic disorder associated with mental retardation and occurs about one in 14,000 births. A child born with PKU has a biochemical defect that prevents him/her from properly metabolizing a substance in protein, called phenylalanine. Consequently, with the ingestion of protein, excessive amounts of phenylalanine accumulate in the body, eventually causing brain damage and mental retardation. Although researchers are not sure precisely how the brain is affected, they know that excessive phenylalanine in the body does cause damage to the baby's fast-growing brain. (Batshaw & Perret, 1981; Koch et al., 1984; Schild, 1964; Waisbren, Schnell & Levy, 1980)

### Etiology

PKU is inherited as an autosomal recessive trait occuring about one in 14,000 births.

### Diagnosis

Shortly after birth, PKU can be detected through a routine screening test called the Guthrie test; the test does not establish the diagnosis, but the results of the test can alert the physician to request further studies to confirm or rule out the diagnosis. At the time of this writing, it is not possible to diagnosis PKU prenatally; however, research now being conducted shows promise that prenatal diagnosis of PKU soon may be available.

### Signs and Symptoms

If untreated, the clinical features of PKU are: mental retardation, hyperactive behavior, depigmentation of the hair and skin, delayed speech, skin rashes, and seizures.

### Mental Retardation

With treatment, mental retardation is not an issue.

### Treatment Concerns

Fortunately, PKU is one of the few such disorders where mental retardation can be appreciably prevented with early identification of the disorder and implementation of appropriate dietary management. Once PKU is diagnosed, treatment should begin immediately, preferably before the third week of life.

The treatment or management of PKU is best carried out in an interdisciplinary setting where the patient's diet can be monitored and where the patient can receive periodic evaluations by medicine, psychology, social work, nutrition, and other disciplines as indicated. In addition to the dietary management of PKU, it is important for the interdisciplinary team to follow the child's developmental progress and to give attention to emotional stresses or special problems that might otherwise arise from the family in the course of care. However, for the patient, dietary management is the method of treatment. To prevent retardation, the basic diet includes a commercially prepared formula of nutritional foods in which most of the phenylalanine has been removed. For younger children, Lofenalac (Mead-Johnson®) is used; for older children, Phenyl-Free (Mead-Johnson®) is recommended along with restricted quantities of high protein foods.

An ever-present issue in the management of PKU is when or at what age to discontinue the diet without affecting the intellectual functioning. At one time, health professionals recommended terminating the diet at 6 to 8 years of age. However, the current thinking is to continue the diet at least through the school-age years, and ideally, into the adult years, especially for females of child bearing age. A summary of 19 published studies directly concerned with the question of diet termination and intellectual levels concluded that with the termination of a phenylalanine-restricted diet, "the performance of some children does not change, whereas the performance of other children decreases substantially." (Waisbren et al., 1980, p. 152)

One of the emerging problems associated with PKU is maternal PKU. Mentally normal females who have PKU are capable of having children but at a risk to the child. Although the child may not have PKU, the child may have mental retardation, heart disease, microcephaly, or low birthweight. Elevated blood levels of phenylalanine in the mother causes increased phenylalanine levels in the fetus and therefore can interfere with normal development. If the PKU mother was on the low-phenylalanine diet before becoming pregnant, and if she continues the diet throughout pregnancy, the chances of having a healthy baby are increased. Any person treated for PKU who plans to have children should seek genetic counseling even though the chances are small that he/she will have a child with the disorder. PKU is an autosomal recessive disorder, which means that an affected person must inherit two defective genes for PKU—one from each parent.

There are several genetic possibilities when one partner has PKU:

1. One partner has PKU; the other is not a carrier. None of the children will have PKU, but all will be carriers.
2. One partner has PKU; the other is a carrier. The chances are fifty-fifty with each pregnancy that the child will have the disorder. If not affected, the child will be a carrier for PKU.
3. Both partners have PKU. All of their children will have PKU.

The role assumed by social work in the management of PKU should take into consideration: (1) the parent's initial reaction to the diagnosis, (2) information-giving after the diagnosis, and (3) support during the dietary management phase. Apparently, the constant self-discipline required to maintain the rigid diet often leads to serious behavioral problems and strains in the parent-child relationship. Schild (1964), in her work with genetic disorders, found that parents of PKU children "reacted to the diagnosis and treatment with overwhelming anxiety, revealing their sense of isolation with the problem" (p. 92). As a result of this observation, she established groups of PKU parents which were designed primarily for supportive and educational purposes but which also provided therapeutic benefits as well. The social worker should recognize that PKU has significant implications for the affected child and the family from birth throughout life and that they will require ongoing support services from a variety of health professionals, including social work.

### Case Study

Mary is a 15½-year-old girl with a diagnosis of PKU. Her first contact for treatment of this disorder occurred when she was 3 weeks old at which time she was placed on a low-phenylalanine diet. Since that time, she has been followed at the Sparks Center on a regular basis, an average of once every three months, by an interdisciplinary team from the Divisions of Nutrition, Medicine, Nursing, Psychology, and Social Work, in order to monitor her diet and to follow her developmental progress. Both of her parents were college graduates. The father was employed as an engineer; the mother did not work outside the home. There was one other child, a boy who was two years older than Mary. The first social work interview did not indicate any major family problems, and both parents seemed to understand the nature of the disorder, its causes and consequences. However, later records indicated that the mother may not have had a full appreciation of the importance of diet management in the treatment of the disorder.

For the first two years, Mary's diet was managed very well. Phenylalanine levels were stabilized, she was growing at a normal rate, her developmental milestones were on time, and her overall general health was good. The first reported problems of adhering to the diet occurred at age 24 months when she started taking food from the refrigerator. From this point on, diet management continued to be a real problem. The mother seemed to have a haphazard approach to enforcing the diet, an attitude which was eventually picked up by Mary.

Age age 6, Mary became even more defiant and for a short period of time discontinued the diet altogether. She experienced sleeping problems and showed irritable-like behavior, both of which continued to be problems. Lab reports from clinic visits also showed that Mary was not following the diet. Phenylalanine levels were consistently above 21 mg when they should have been between 2 and 10 mg. Her academic performance began to decline.

At a parent conference, Mary's parents were told that her IQ had dropped significantly between 1974 and 1982. The correlation of this IQ drop with repeatedly high levels of phenylalanine was discussed. The treatment team further emphasized that the high levels also could contribute to her distractibility and inability to concentrate. She was enrolled in a regular class but was receiving LD services for deficits in math and English. When Mary reached the adolescent years, she was counseled by nursing and social work about the possible problems of maternal PKU. Although at the time she was 13 years of age, all agreed that it was a subject that should be openly discussed; the mother agreed. Mary stated that she had been thinking about the problem and did not know what she would do about ever having children.

During her last visit, the physician had a long talk with the mother and Mary, explaining that Mary's drop in intellectual functioning probably was related to the inadequate diet management. This admonishment did not get results, either.

## Argininosuccinic Aciduria

Argininosuccinic aciduria, the second most common of the urea cycle disorders, is an inborn error of metabolism and is manifested by a variable clinical picture. Common features found in the disorder are mental retardation, seizures, liver disease, and poorly pigmented, brittle hair.

Death occurs during the neonatal period if the disorder is the malignant or early onset type. The incidence of the disorder has been reported as one in 70,000 to one in 160,000 births. (Menkes, 1985; Rudolph, 1982; Smith, 1978)

### Etiology

The disorder is transmitted as an autosomal recessive trait.

### Diagnosis

Affected individuals excrete large quantities of argininosuccinic acid in the urine which can be detected by amino acid chromatography. High concentrations of argininosuccinic acid also are found in the cerebrospinal fluid. The disorder has been diagnosed prenatally.

### Signs and Symptoms

The early or malignant type of this disorder accounts for about 25 percent of the cases. As it develops in the early months of life, affected infants have poor feeding, with vomiting, seizures, and respiratory distress, and generally die within two weeks. With the late-onset type, symptoms are similar but progression is not as rapid. However, the symptoms are mental retardation, irritability, feeding problems, psychomotor delays, seizures, and poorly pigmented, brittle hair. Many individuals are small for their age.

### Mental Retardation

About 20 percent of all affected individuals have normal intelligence. Some show nothing more than learning problems.

### Treatment Concerns

Treatment is directed toward the prevention of hyperammonemia. Long-term treatment calls for a protein-restricted diet supplemented with arginine sodium benzoate and essential amino acids. Other types of intervention depend on the level of retardation (if present), the medical status of the patient, speech and language development, and the ability of the family to cope with the disorder.

### Case Study

Joey, age 3 years 9 months, was referred to the center for evaluations of his hearing, speech, and general developmental status. The referring pediatrician specifically requested help in "coordinating an overall plan and approach to Joey's care." Laboratory studies at 18 months already had confirmed the diagnosis of argininosuccinic aciduria. A physical examination revealed tracheal malacia (softness of the tracheal tissue); coarse, sparse hair, curvature of the fingers (clinodactyly); low-set ears; and growth retardation. According to developmental testing, he was 1½ to 2 years delayed. He had a moderate to severe hearing loss and significant delays in speech and language. A leg-length discrepancy was noted.

The social work interview found that Joey's family was a low-income family of four living in a rural area where unemployment rates were high. The father, age 40, was a machine operator in a plant that manufactured chairs; however, this employment had been irregular. Although they were eligible for food stamps, they received no aid except for help with school lunches. Joey was on Medicaid. The mother, age 32, was not employed outside the home, because she felt that the demands of Joey's care precluded it. She was almost "house bound" because of her great fear that something would happen to Joey while at school and she would not be right there to help him. She had little respite from his care and rarely went out, because she did not trust most babysitters. This also restricted Joey's social environment, in that, aside from school, he had few experiences with persons and situations beyond home and the immediate family.

What was important to note, however, was the profound psychosocial effect that these disabilities had on this child and parents in their daily functioning. First of all, Joey had been hospitalized about once a month ever since birth; this amounted to 36 or so hospital admissions. Ordinarily, mild illnesses such as diarrhea, colds and ear infections induced a severe reaction, causing him to have high fevers, to turn blue, and to generally become acutely ill as the ammonia levels in his blood began to rise. Apparently, on some occasions, his life had been in question and the parents have even wondered if he would live to see another birthday.

All of this had had a curious effect on family life, and the fear that something would happen had severely limited the opportunity of the mother either to work or to pursue her own interests. Additionally, the parents had become overly protective, in that they really did not seem to discipline Joey at all and were constantly concerned about his well-being. The social worker commented that it was rather typical to see parents who expected too much, but these parents were expecting too little, with the result that Joey was less mature and capable than he could be. The parents needed education and reassurance in this area.

The parents stated that they understood the metabolic condition and did not find managing the diet too much of a problem; under the supervision of a nutritionist, a special diet was prescribed. The fact that he had a small trachea that closed up easily if he cried influenced the parents not to discipline him too much for fear that he might cry and then stop breathing, which apparently already had happened a few times. Other problems with Joey's physical condition that concerned the family were his hearing loss, his lack of speech, enuresis, and orthopedic problems. The social worker's impressions and evaluation stated that the family certainly had some strengths or they would not have survived so much illness and hardship so well. However, some recommendations were made which included support of the parents in developing some realistic expectations of the child beyond the mere survival stage; the possible need for respite care services; and encouraging the parents to apply for SSI monthly benefits and food stamps.

## Galactosemia

Galactosemia, an inborn error of metabolism, is caused by a deficiency of the enzyme required to convert galactose (a simple sugar the body cannot use) to glucose (a simple sugar which the body cells can use). Consequently, the body cannot use galactose or lactose, which is milk sugar. About 1 percent of the population carries the trait for the disorder, and the incidence of galactosemia is about one in 40,000 births. (Batshaw & Perret, 1981; Cassells & Vermeersch, 1976; Wenz & Michell, 1978)

### Etiology

The disorder follows the autosomal recessive mode of inheritance.

### Diagnosis

Screening for galactosemia is not done routinely in some states. If the disorder is suspected, testing is done through a urine or blood test. Prenatal diagnosis by analysis of the amniotic fluid is available.

## Signs and Symptoms

If untreated, symptoms begin to appear within a few days after milk feeding—breast milk or infant formula. Affected infants fail to grow and gain weight; they may have diarrhea, stomach bloating, vomiting, cataracts, and generally may act lethargic. Significant mental retardation occurs in most infants who are not treated before one month of age. Without treatment, the child commonly dies from infection or liver failure.

## Mental Retardation

Without treatment before one month of age, mental retardation will result.

## Treatment Concerns

The treatment of galactosemia is not a difficult or complicated task, but the patient must adhere to a galactose-restricted diet which excludes milk products and other sources of lactose, including organ meats and certain vegetables containing lactose. Infants are given a substitute of soy formulas. As the child grows, dietary management is recommended along with periodic nutritional counseling. Since the disorder is inherited as an autosomal recessive trait, genetic counseling is recommended. Otherwise, the patient is best treated by an interdisciplinary team that takes into account his/her dietary needs and developmental progress as well as the family's overall adjustment to problems associated with galactosemia.

## Case Study

At 11 weeks of age, Sean was referred by his physician to a university center for evaluation of hepatomegaly (enlarged liver).

The child was the third pregnancy of a 22-year-old mother. Birthweight was at the 75th percentile (above average). He had no overt problems and was discharged after one day on infant formula. At about 2 weeks of age, he began vomiting. At 2 months of age, when he was hospitalized for otitis media, his weight was at the 10th percentile (well below average) and he was anemic.

Findings upon hospital admission were hepatomegaly, failure to thrive, cataracts, decreased muscle tone, and a negative test for glucose oxidase in the urine. The diagnostic impression was possible galactosemia—most likely glucose-1-phosphate uridyl transferase deficiency (classic galactosemia). Two days before discharge, the infant was started on a lactose-free diet in which Isomil®, a soy formula, was substituted for milk. The urine-reducing substances disappeared and he gained weight. The diagnosis of galactosemia was made.

At 2 years 8 months of age, the child was seen at Sparks Center. Physical examination was normal with no evidence of hepatomegaly. Weight/height relationship was slightly above the 75th percentile (above average weight for height). Psychological testing placed him within the low-average range of intelligence. Parents reported that he had developed normally. He had cataracts and was continuing a galactose-restricted diet. The plan of the Sparks Center staff was to monitor his galactose level, perform periodic medical, psychologic and social work evaluations, and provide dietary counseling.

## Seckel Syndrome (Nanocephalic Dwarfism)

Seckel syndrome is characterized by proportionate dwarfism, a small, "bird-like" appearing head, and mental retardation which may vary from mild to severe. Birthweight is usually below 5 pounds and the patient may remain slender. The head circumference of newborns is as small as 27 cm (normal: 34–35 cm); for adults, head circumference may be 39–45 cm (normal: 55–56 cm) (Gorlin et al., 1976). The beak-like protrusion of the central part of the face (prominent nose and receding chin) gives an "aztec-like appearance." (Gorlin et al., 1976; Lemeshow, 1982)

### Etiology

The disorder is probably transmitted as an autosomal recessive trait.

### Diagnosis

The diagnosis is based on the clinical findings.

### Signs and Symptoms

Proportionate dwarfism, widely set eyes (hypertelorism); antimongoloid slant of eyes; epicanthal fold (extra fold at inner corner of the eyes); lobeless, low-set ears; small jaw (micrognathia); possible cleft palate and/or high palate vault; anomalies of the genitalia and urinary tract; possible abnormalities of pigmentation; excessive hair (hypertrichosis); and numerous skeletal anomalies.

## Mental Retardation

Mental development rarely surpasses the five-year-old level.

## Treatment Concerns

The major treatment concerns are: Genetic counseling for the parents; supportive counseling for the parents; special education placement based on the level of retardation of the affected individual; possible speech therapy; orthopedic care for abnormalities of the skeletal system; and, for the severely retarded, an adaptive developmental program with an emphasis on self-help skills and language stimulation.

## Case Study

Sharon was 19 months of age when a neurologist referred her to the Sparks Center. At the time, a diagnosis of Seckel bird-headed dwarfism was suspected. (The previously suspected chromosome 13 aberration was ruled out by the Laboratory of Medical Genetics in 1981.)

The mother, age 22, was employed as a factory worker in a small plant. (It was noted that the mother had hypopigmented areas on her face and arms.) The father was blind due to an automobile accident when he was 21 years of age. He was employed by the Industries for the Blind. They met while both were attending a vocational rehabilitation program.

Sharon was a full-term baby weighing only 4 pounds 2 ounces. She was born without thumbs and had a very small head and numerous other congenital anomalies, including a cleft palate. A few days after birth, she was transferred to a high-risk nursery at the medical center where she remained several weeks. She then was transferred back to her local hospital where she stayed for about a month. Upon reaching 5 pounds, Sharon was released from the hospital. Because of the physical anomalies and her failure to thrive, Sharon was brought to the Laboratory of Medical Genetics, University of Alabama at Birmingham. The results of this visit indicated that Sharon had a normal female karotype with no chromosomal defects. The diagnosis of Seckel bird-headed dwarfism was explained to the mother, but she and her husband still did not understand the significance of the diagnosis.

The results of the evaluations at the Sparks Center were: severe mental retardation; confirmation of the diagnosis of Seckel syndrome; below the 5th percentile in height, weight and head circumference; and small mouth with malformed teeth and cleft palate. From these results, the following recommendations were made: (1) referral to an orthopedic speciality clinic; (2) referral to State Crippled Children Service Cleft Palate Clinic; (3) referral to the WIC nutrition program; (4) routine eye exams on a yearly basis; (5) genetic counseling; and (6) dietary counseling. The social worker stated: "I see this couple as desperately needing some understanding about Sharon's problems and what they can expect in the future as far as intellectual capabilities are concerned. No one has been very effective in interpreting information to the parents about their daughter's diagnosis, and subsequent appointments were made to see that they understood the diagnosis and its consequences."

## AUTOSOMAL DOMINANT DISORDERS

Autosomal dominant disorders differ from autosomal recessive disorders in several ways. The primary difference is that only one defective gene, instead of two, is required to produce the disorder. The harmful gene is dominant. This means that an individual who has an autosomal dominant disorder stands a fifty-fifty chance of giving the defective gene to his/her offspring. Another characteristic is that with dominant disorders, traits may be expressed in degrees of severity varying widely from person to person. This situation is referred to as reduced penetrance and variable expressivity. With dominant disorders, diagnosis is difficult because sometimes individuals are only mildly affected. Mental retardation occurs concomitantly with relatively few dominant disorders as compared to recessive disorders.

Approximately 1,500 autosomal dominant disorders are confirmed or suspected to date. Examples of dominant disorders include Huntington's chorea, a progressive degeneration of the nervous system; achondroplasia, a form of dwarfism; and osteogenesis imperfecta, a disorder characterized by brittle bones. Tuberous sclerosis is an example of a dominant disorder in which mental retardation can be a factor.

### Apert Syndrome (Acrocephalosyndactyly)

Apert syndrome, an inherited disorder, is typified by a high, peaked skull (acrocephaly) and fused fingers and toes (syndactyly). Orthopedic problems, varying in severity, may be associated with the disorder. The frequency of Apert syndrome is about one in 160,000 births, but the high mortality rate in the neonatal period decreases its prevalence significantly. (Gorlin et al., 1976; Lemeshow, 1982)

### Etiology

The disorder is suspected to follow the autosomal dominant type of inheritance, with most cases representing a new mutation.

### Diagnosis

The diagnosis is based on the clinical findings.

### Signs and Symptoms

Among the craniofacial features found are: a full forehead and flat occiput (back of the head); irregular craniosynostosis (union of bones by osseous tissues) eventually causing a dome-shaped head; flat facies; bulging and widely set eyes; down-slanting palpebral fissures; flat nasal bridge with a "beak-like" appearance; underdeveloped upper jaw; and low-set ears.

Defects of the skeletal system include: total to partial fusion of fingers and toes which result in a "mitten hand" and "sock foot" appearance, and fusing (ankylosing) of the vertebrae of the back, and of other joints.

Vision problems and/or hearing loss are common. The mouth, usually small, may have a high-arched palate and crowded teeth.

### Mental Retardation

Some degree of mental retardation is found in most patients. Normal intelligence has been observed in some patients.

### Treatment Concerns

The disorder will require early medical attention to separate webbed fingers and toes. If intracranial pressure is evident, surgery for craniosynostosis is indicated. Other orthopedic problems will call for special appliances and therapy to assist the patient with mobility. Because of structural defects of the mouth and crowded teeth, dental care and speech therapy may have a high priority in the treatment process. The impact of the diagnosis on the family, which is usually evident at birth, is often severe, and many parents will need information and support during this time. Long-term intervention may be indicated when parents are not coping effectively and where they are having difficulty locating services. As the child grows older, he/she may need special education placement based on intellectual capabilities.

## Case Study

Michael, a 4-year-old male with Apert syndrome, was referred to the Sparks Center by a pediatrician for early intervention services. At birth, he was noted to have multiple anomalies consistent with Apert syndrome which was confirmed with the following findings supporting the diagnosis: syndactyly of the hands and feet, tall forehead, hypertelorism, small nose, mild micrognathia, high-arched palate, simplified low-set ears, down-slanting palpebral fissures, and shallow orbits. Skull x-rays revealed premature closure of the coronal sutures. His physical condition was stable at birth and, with the exception of hyperbilirubinemia, treated with phototherapy; there were no complications. He underwent surgery at approximately 2 months of age for the craniosynostosis, and further hand surgery was to be scheduled.

Both parents were in their late twenties, had professional jobs, and seemed to have an excellent understanding of Apert syndrome. There were no other children, but they planned to have additional children despite the recurrence risk of having another child with Apert syndrome.

The social worker believed that the strengths in the marital relationship, the parents' knowledge of the disorder, and resources available to them should enable them to deal satisfactorily with the stresses and challenges of raising a child with this disorder. The parents were aware that he was at risk for developmental delays or mental retardation. Nevertheless, it was felt that they would benefit from ongoing support and guidance, plus an early developmental program for Michael.

## Tuberous Sclerosis Syndrome

Tuberous sclerosis includes congenital lesions of the skin and of the central nervous system. It is characterized by (a) epilepsy, (b) mental retardation, and (c) cutaneous angiofibromas (tumors consisting of fibrous tissue). Some of the signs can be present at birth (e.g. hypopigmented skin spots). However, the majority of patients have seizures and skin changes beginning at ages 2 to 6 years. The syndrome is found in about one in 100,000 to 200,000 in the general population. (Behrman & Vaughan, 1983; Gorlin et al., 1976; Smith, 1982)

### *Etiology*

The disorder follows the autosomal dominant mode of inheritance with variable expressivity. The disorder may vary markedly in severity with some individuals being severely involved and others normal. About 80 percent of the cases represent fresh mutations from unaffected parents.

### *Diagnosis*

The diagnosis is based on the clinical findings.

### *Signs and Symptoms*

Convulsions, occurring in more than 90 percent of the patients, are the most common clinical signs of brain involvement. Myoclonic seizures may occur during the first few years of life; grand mal and psychomotor seizures predominate later. About 50 percent of the patients have intracranial calcification.

Adenoma sebaceum (tumor-like growths), varying in color from flesh to bright red to brown, is the most characteristic skin lesion of the disorder. These lesions, which usually appear from 2 to 5 years of age, are found in a "butterfly" distribution on the nose and cheeks. By late childhood they are found in more than 80 percent of the patients.

Hypopigmented macules (white spots) on the skin of the arms, legs and trunk may be present from birth. The size of these spots varies from millimeters to centimeters in diameter. They have an oval or irregular outline. Hypopigmented hairs are sometimes present within them.

Fibrous tumors (fibromas) may be found at the base of the fingernails, toenails, or on the forehead and scalp. Shagreen patches (slightly raised, hard areas of skin) are often found over the back. "Cafe au lait" spots (light brown in color) are present in about 7 percent of the cases.

### *Mental Retardation*

Varying from mild to severe, mental retardation is present in 60 percent to 70 percent of patients. Behavior disorders, especially hyperactivity and destructiveness, are common.

### *Treatment Concerns*

The prognosis is variable. Some patients who are mildly affected may enjoy full, productive lives and have severely affected children. For the severely retarded, institutionalization may be required. Early death may be due to status epilepticus, brain tumor, renal failure or tumor of the heart. Medical care includes genetic counseling, management of seizures, possible surgery to remove tumors, and visual care for cataracts and optic lesions. Careful psychological testing will determine educational needs. Parents should benefit from long-term, supportive counseling to help them deal with the complications and stresses that might be imposed by the presence of the disorder.

## Case Study

At 6 months of age, Mary was diagnosed as having a brain tumor, which turned out to be a symptom of tuberous sclerosis. She was treated with medication for seizure activity. Although she apparently was doing well on medication, several months later she again began having seizures which occurred on a daily basis for a three- or four-month period. These lasted for only a few minutes but occurred as frequently as several times a day every day despite the medication. The neurologist suspected that she might be mentally slow and referred her to the Sparks Center for further evaluations.

The mother was interviewed. She immediately emphasized that she did not plan to have any more children and run a risk of having another child with tuberous sclerosis. The mother was an attractive, verbal individual who obviously was very distressed. She said her husband was extremely supportive and that their marriage had been strengthened by Mary and her handicaps. The mother seemed to have some knowledge of tuberous sclerosis, but several questions remained unanswered because so much information had been given to her by so many sources. She was optimistic about the prognosis and felt that if Mary could talk, she could make many other advancements in development. Self-help skills were poor; she could not dress or feed herself, nor was she toilet trained (age 3 years). The parents' social life had been limited, in that they could not locate babysitters because everyone was fearful of the seizures. For this reason a local church would not accept Mary into the "mother's day out" program. The mother stressed that her every waking moment was spent thinking or worrying about Mary.

Findings from the evaluations were severe mental retardation, intracranial calcification, fibromas around fingernails and scalp, inflamed gums, small size (below 5th percentile for height and weight), astigmatism in the right eye, simple hyperopia in the left eye, and delays in gross motor functions. Eventually, Mary was placed in a multiply handicapped program. Counseling for the parents was provided to give them complete information about the disorder and to assist them in dealing with the emotional stress that was quite severe, especially for the mother.

## Neurofibromatosis Syndrome (von Recklinghausen Disease)

Neurofibromatosis is a genetic disease that affects the skin as well as the nervous system. Estimates indicate that the incidence of the disorder in the general population is one in 3,000. (Crowe, Schull & Neel, 1952; Ford, 1966; Menkes, 1985; Smith, 1982)

### *Etiology*

The disorder follows the autosomal dominant type of inheritance, with approximately one-half of the cases representing new mutations.

### *Diagnosis*

The presence of six or more cafe-au-lait spots (one centimeter or more in diameter) is helpful in making the diagnosis, but more spots may develop over a period of time. In some cases, the diagnosis is more difficult because superficial lesions are absent.

### *Signs and Symptoms*

The syndrome has variable manifestations from patient to patient; therefore, a complete clinical description is complex. Some individuals are mildly affected, and they may never be diagnosed, or the symptoms of the disorder may evolve slowly. About 40 percent of affected individuals show some of the symptoms at birth; more than 60 percent show signs by the second year. Cutaneous skin tumors called neurofibromata, which are most often benign, are the most striking and common feature. The tumors may be present at birth, may appear during childhood or even later, and may involve the stomach, intestine, kidney, bladder, larynx or heart. They vary greatly in size and can grow anywhere in the body. If they grow large enough to put pressure on and destroy a vital nerve, serious damage can result, especially if the brain or spinal cord is affected. The potential exists for blindness, deafness, and other crippling conditions. Also, patients are at risk to develop malignant tumors.

The cafe-au-lait spots occur in about 90 percent of the patients. Axillary (armpit) freckling is present in approximately one-third of the cases. Seizures frequently are associated with the disorder also.

### Mental Retardation

Mental retardation is present in about 10 percent to 15 percent of affected individuals. The level of retardation is usually mild to moderate.

### Treatment Concerns

Depending on the location of the tumors, the prognosis for most affected individuals in generally good. The possibility of malignant changes should be of concern, and surgery may be necessary when intracranial or intraspinal tumors are present. Because of the fear of causing malignant changes, treatment may be reduced or limited as much as possible. It is best for patients to select a physician who is knowledgeable about the disorder and also familiar with resources that are helpful in the management of the disorder (i.e. neurology, orthopedics, and genetics). In view of the manner in which the disorder is transmitted, genetic services are indicated for both the patient and parents. Patients are advised to have, on a yearly basis, hearing and visual exams, blood pressure checks, and examinations of the back for possible scoliosis (curvature of the spine).

### Case Study

Melissa, a 10-year-old girl, had a record of poor achievement in school. Also, she demonstrated overall developmental delays and very low self-esteem. Her teacher, who referred her to the Sparks Center for a comprehensive evaluation, described her as having speech problems and performing poorly in physical activities. Melissa was tested in 1979, and on the Stanford-Binet she scored at the borderline mental retardation level. On physical exam, she had numerous cafe-au-lait spots, and the examination confirmed the previous diagnosis of neurofibromatosis.

Melissa came from a low-income, single-parent family of two. The mother, the sole support of the household, had an extremely busy schedule. She had a full-time job as an LPN at the V.A. Hospital and a weekend job at a nursing home; at the same time, she was enrolled in a degree-granting nursing program at a local college. All this activity left her with little time for leisure and with very little time for Melissa, who spent much time with the maternal grandmother. Melissa's parents were not married, but, until the father's death (following a head injury in an accidental fall), the father was said to have spent a good deal of time with her and she was quite depressed when he died. The mother stated that she did not plan to marry, because she felt the genetic question regarding the heritability of neurofibromatosis would be a problem. The diagnosis was explained to her, but it was clear that she did not have an accurate notion of the genetic factors involved and that this needed to be clarified for her peace of mind. Melissa was aware of the diagnosis of neurofibromatosis and, though the consequences had been explained to her, she still wondered if she would die soon. She already had made other comments related to death and dying; in addition, she exhibited many of the symptoms commonly associated with depression. The social worker felt that she was an extremely lonely girl. The worker comments: "It is my impression that this litle girl, in addition to having neurofibromatosis, is also suffering the depressing effects of living a socially isolated, lonely life-style which is devoid of many of the usual pleasures of childhood. Also, circumstances, along with other things, have led her to have almost no age peer friends and to be growing up almost exclusively in the company of her somewhat withdrawn mother and her aging grandmother."

Several recommendations were made, primarily ways to improve Melissa's environment so that it contained some of the pleasant socially stimulating elements of a normal childhood. In addition, the genetic aspects of neurofibromatosis needed to be explained so that the mother could have a realistic basis for deciding if she wanted to have additional children and for determining what the risks for Melissa's children might be. Having accurate information on the recurrence risk might prevent this mother from unduly limiting her social life, as was the case. Medically, Melissa needed annual formal hearing and visual tests, as well as a yearly general neurological and physical exam to check especially for signs of scoliosis.

## X-LINKED DISORDERS

Females have two X chromosomes; males have one X and one Y chromosome. By having one X chromosome, males stand a 100 percent chance of manifesting X-linked disorders when a mutant, recessive gene is located on the X chromosome. This condition occurs because males have no matched gene to counteract the harmful effects of the recessive gene on the X chromosome. To date no defective genes have been found on the Y chromosome. Most often, females who have a recessive gene on one of their X chromosomes function as normal carriers, because they have a matched X with "normal" genes to dominate.

In cases of X-linked recessive disorders, it is the mother who gives the mutant, recessive gene to her sons, each of whom has a fifty-fifty chance of inheriting the disorder. Each of her daughters has a fifty-fifty chance of inheriting the defective gene also, but they are carriers for the disorder.

Fathers do not give their sons an X chromosome; therefore, an affected father cannot transmit an X-linked recessive disorder to his sons, but he will give the recessive gene to all his daughters who will be carriers for the disorder. Males are never carriers for an X-linked disorder; they are either XY normal or affected. Females rarely are affected by an X-linked disorder.

Approximately 200 disorders are X-linked recessive. Some examples of known X-linked recessive conditions are hemophilia, Duchenne muscular dystrophy, color blindness, and a type of hydrocephalus. Hunter and Lesch-Nyhan syndromes are two X-linked disorders that involve mental retardation.

## COFFIN-LOWRY SYNDROME

Coffin-Lowry syndrome is an inherited disorder with characteristic facies, bony abnormalities and mental retardation; the expression is more pronounced in males than in females. (Gorlin, 1981; Hunter, Partington & Evans, 1982; Smith, 1982)

### Etiology

X-linked inheritance is suggested by the fact that males are more severely affected than females.

### Diagnosis

Minimal diagnostic criteria: craniofacial defects, severe mental retardation, short stature, and hand anomalies.

## Signs and Symptoms

The face has a coarse appearance with a square forehead, down-slanting palpebral fissures, a broad nasal bridge, hypertelorism, prominent eyes, and thick, pouting lips. A high and narrow palate may be present; teeth may be small or missing. Growth deficiency is of postnatal onset. Other musculoskeletal abnormalities include: large soft hands with tapering fingers; flat feet; lax ligaments; thoracolumbar kyphoscoliosis (lateral curvature of the spine with anteroposterior hump); or lordosis ("swayback"); short bifid sternum with pectus carinatum (keel-shaped); or pectus excavatum (depressed). Hernias and various dermatoglyphic alterations are found frequently.

## Mental Retardation

Affected males generally have IQs less than 50.

## Treatment Concerns

Management of the disorder begins with helping the parents understand and adjust to the diagnosis. The mode of inheritance, X-linked, reflects the need for extensive genetic counseling for all family members. Early intervention programs are useful in stimulating maximum development in infants; special education classes should be based on the child's intellectual functioning. During adolescence and early adulthood, a sheltered work situation in the open community may be helpful. Patients often benefit from management by an entire team of specialists (i.e. physicians, speech pathologists, audiologists, physical and occupational therapists, social workers, and teachers).

## Case Study

Tim, age 16, was mentally retarded, a condition that had been apparent throughout his life. However, a true assessment of his handicaps had never been completed, nor had the etiology of his disabilities ever been determined. Developmental delays were noted by his parents in early infancy, but he had received no intervention prior to entering school at age 7. Psychometric testing by the school indicated that he was functioning within the severe range of mental retardation. His language was significantly delayed. He had been placed in a multiply handicapped class where he had remained throughout his school career. He was somewhat difficult to manage, but the parents recognized that he would never reach a level of complete independence.

During an on-site visit to the school by the State Department of Education, a question was raised regarding the appropriateness of his placement. A TMR class with children at his age level was suggested, but this class was about 18 miles from his home. The parents were opposed to any changes without further diagnostic work. Consequently, a referral was made to the Sparks Center for a comprehensive evaluation.

The clinical findings of severe mental retardation and short stature, characteristic craniofacial defects, and large soft hands with tapering fingers suggested a diagnosis of Coffin-Lowry syndrome. Other findings included significant language delays, dental anomalies with poor oral hygiene, and inadequate caloric and protein intake. He was below the 5th percentile for height and weight. Genetic counseling was recommended for the parents even though they did not plan to have additional children. A pedigree of extended family members was obtained to help identify potential carriers of the disorder who in turn would need genetic counseling.

Both parents were employed at a textile mill. Tim had two older brothers; a 20-year-old brother resided in the household. The brother had prostheses of the lower extremities (these extremeties had been amputated because of congenital defects), but he experienced few physical limitations and was the source of enormous help in the care of Tim. He attended trade school but would soon leave home to work in another state as a mechanic. Tim's 18-year-old brother, a recent high-school graduate, was a construction worker and visited the family on weekends. Several concerns regarding the family situation emerged from the social work interview. The parents were concerned about the changes in educational placement which seemed so unnecessary and were viewed by them as a ploy "to get rid of Tim." Additionally, the two brothers who had reached adulthood were no longer in the home and could no longer assist in the care and management of Tim. Therefore, the mother planned to quit her job to assume his full-time care. This would mean a substantial loss in income, but no other solutions seemed possible.

Through much effort, the social worker located a day-care center for Tim which enabled the mother to continue working. Earlier, Tim had not qualified for SSI, but the parents were advised to apply again when he reached 18 years old, at which time he should qualify for SSI benefits regardless of the family's income.

# HUNTER SYNDROME (MUCOPOLYSACCHARIDOSIS II)

Hunter syndrome is a biochemical disease in which there is an accumulation in certain parts of the body of mucopolysaccharides that eventually cause mental retardation, possible cardiac failure, limitation of movement, enlargement of the liver and spleen, and the likelihood of death before age 20. The onset of the abnormalities is at 2 to 4 years of age. The disorder manifests in both mild and severe forms. The frequency of Hunter syndrome is estimated to be less than one in 100,000. (Gellis, Feingold & Rutman, 1968; Gorlin et al., 1976; Smith, 1982)

## Etiology

Hunter syndrome is X-linked recessive. Carrier females have with each pregnancy a fifty-fifty chance of their sons being affected, and fifty-fifty chance of their daughters being carriers.

## Diagnosis

The affected male and carrier female can be detected through biochemical studies. The affected male also can be detected prenatally.

## Signs and Symptoms

The outstanding features of Hunter syndrome are: short stature, coarse facial features, enlarged head, thick lips, and large tongue. Patients may have visual problems and/or progressive nerve deafness. The abdomen tends to be enlarged because of enlarged liver and spleen. The joints may be stiff, and the hands may show a "claw-like" appearance with short, stubby fingers. A gradual decline in the growth rate occurs from 2 to 6 years of age.

## Mental Retardation

Mild retardation usually is seen in the mild or late type of Hunter syndrome.

## Treatment Concerns

Special education may help those who fall within the mildly retarded range. The severely retarded will require trainable classes. Physical therapy should be initiated to avoid contractures as much as possible. Also, vision and hearing problems may require special attention. Genetic counseling to help the family understand the diagnosis, prognosis and risk factors are essential. Another component of any effective long-range treatment plan is to provide, if at all possible through social work, a means of helping the family work through their emotional reactions which may be the most difficult challenge in the treatment process.

## Case Study

At age 9, Ricky was suspected of having a mental retardation disorder and was referred to the Sparks Center. On physical exam, he manifested many of the characteristics of Hunter syndrome: coarsening of facial features; microcephaly; broad hands and feet; clinodactyly; growth deficiency; temporal bulging; puffiness of the upper eyelids; hypertelorism; depressed nasal bridge; and borderline mental retardation. On the WISC-R, he obtained a score of 70. At 1 year of age, Ricky had been placed in a foster home after a welfare department investigation found evidence of neglect. His mentally retarded mother was not capable of providing adequate care. Almost no background information was available. However, there was a history of two maternal uncles who reportedly had Hunter syndrome; one uncle died at the age of 17 and the other at age 28.

During the time Ricky stayed in a foster home, his developmental milestones were reported to be somewhat delayed. He had poor coordination and needed much extra help with almost every task. He had a tendency to develop frequent colds with high fevers and a "croupy" cough. The State Crippled Children Service followed him for orthopedic problems, and eventually corrective shoes were prescribed. Ricky needed frequent dental care for inflamed gums and other dental problems. The foster mother observed that he had many unusual fears such as being terrified of lightning, thunder, the wind, and strangers. In fact, these fears became so severe that treatment at a local mental health agency was necessary.

At age 3 years 3 months, Ricky was adopted by a middle-class family who had specifically requested a handicapped child. They were aware that Ricky had some problems, but he turned out to be more of a challenge than they had anticipated. Over the years, behavior had been the major issue. The mother thought that his behavioral problems were related to the fact that his appearance distinguished him from his peers, and that his awareness of this difference resulted in inappropriate behavior. At 18 years of age, he had two years remaining in school and was enrolled in an emotional conflict class. He had gained considerable weight and had visual problems as well as many allergy problems. The parents were concerned about his behavior (which they believed could lead to serious legal problems), his vocational future, and the likelihood of death prior to his reaching adulthood.

## Chapter Six

# MULTIFACTORIAL DISORDERS

D ISORDERS thought to be caused by a combination of genetic and
environmental factors are termed "multifactorial." A neural tube
defect (e.g. spina bifida) is caused by a failure of the neural tube to close
properly early in pregnancy and is an example of a multifactorial disorder. Cleft lip and/or palate, club foot, congenital dislocation of the hip,
and pyloric stenosis are examples of conditions that are thought to be
due to multifactorial inheritance. From the multifactorial group of disorders, one syndrome, spina bifida, is selected for discussion along with
a case history.

## SPINA BIFIDA

The term "spina bifida" (*bifid* = split in two) refers to open defects in
the spinal canal. There are three types of spina bifida. The most severe
type is called myelomeningocele (*myelo* = cord; *meninges* = covering of the
spinal cord; *cele* = sac), in which the spinal cord protrudes from some
point on the back into a membranous sac (the skin may not completely
cover the protrusion). With meningocele only the membranes surrounding the spinal cord (not the cord itself) protrude. The least severe of the
three types of open spine defects is spina bifida occulta which may go
unnoticed in some cases or which may have an overlying midline patch
of hair or birthmark. The incidence of spina bifida is between 0.1 and
4.13 of 1,000 live births. (Anderson & Spain, 1977; Bleck & Nagel,
1975; Myers, Cerone, & Olson, 1981)

### Etiology

Spina bifida, one of the neural tube defects, is due to abnormal development of the spinal canal originating early in pregnancy. The reason

for this abnormal development is unknown, but investigators believe it is caused by a combination of genetic and environmental influences. Consequently, it is classified as a multifactorial disorder.

## Diagnosis

Open spina bifida is obvious at birth. Prenatal diagnosis is available. If the back of the fetus is open during the prenatal stage, a protein called alpha-fetoprotein leaks out into the amniotic fluid. Through amniocentesis this fluid can be analyzed to determine whether the fetus has an open spine defect. The test is accurate in about 90 percent to 95 percent of cases.

Prenatally, a screening test can measure the amount of alpha-fetoprotein in the mother's blood. This screening test is not always accurate, but preliminary results can help the physician determine whether additional testing is indicated. The maternal alpha-fetoprotein screening results in a large number of false positives, about 50 per 1,000.

## Signs and Symptoms

Some of the conditions associated with myelomeningocele are: hydrocephalus; loss of motor control (paralysis), especially in the legs; sensory loss in the area of paralysis; lack of bladder and bowel control (incontinence); deformities of the spine and limbs; dislocation of the hips; and strabismus.

## Mental Retardation

Among children with spina bifida, only about one-third are mentally retarded. However, some children with spina bifida have hyperverbal behavior, often described as "the cocktail party syndrome." This behavior sometimes can give the false impression that the child's intellectual functioning is high.

## Treatment Concerns

The primary treatment issues of spina bifida are:

1. Problems of the open spine;
2. Hydrocephalus;
3. Bladder and bowel dysfunction;
4. Bone deformities;
5. Psychosocial problems.

The first medical problem requiring attention is the back. Although closure of the back is not immediately necessary, every effort should be made to prevent infections. If the sac is open, torn, or ruptured, the nervous system can be exposed and the child will be vulnerable to infections such as meningitis. Once the sac is surgically closed, the survival rate of children with spina bifida is increased greatly.

About 65 percent to 70 percent of children with spina bifida develop hydrocephalus (*hydro* = water; *cephalus* = head), a condition in which excessive cerebral spinal fluid (CSF) builds up in the ventricles within the brain. If the disorder is not treated, pressure from the fluid can cause permanent brain damage and mental retardation. A system of tubes and valves, called a ventriculo-peritoneal (VP) shunt, provides a pathway for the fluid to flow from the brain to the peritoneal cavity in the abdomen where the fluid is then absorbed by the body.

In the past, kidney infections have been a major problem for patients with spina bifida. However, better management techniques have reduced urinary tract infections and made a significant difference in the long-term survival of these patients. Most children with myelomeningocele have neurogenic bladders (a lack of control of the urinary sphincter) and this can lead to kidney damage.

Deformities of the feet and knees or a dislocated hip are present in some patients and may require therapy or even surgery. Curvature of the spine (*kyphosis* = forward curvature of the spine; *scoliosis* = lateral curvature) can be a problem in spina bifida. If one of the types of curvature is present, bracing or surgery may be necessary. Additionally, with spina bifida the patient may be confined to a wheelchair, and if there is a deformity in the back, special problems with positioning can occur.

The spina bifida child is more vulnerable to psychosocial problems than other children. Emotional and behavioral problems manifested by some children with spina bifida are thought to be related to the situations listed below.

1. Frequent and prolonged hospitalizations;
2. Inability to compete, academically in some cases;
3. A sense of being different;
4. Problems of bladder and bowel control;
5. Physical limitations and social isolation;
6. Distractibility, a fairly common characteristic of children with neurological abnormalities.
7. Dependence upon adults, especially during the early years;
8. Loss of motivation and passivity;

9. Fears and anxieties (about themselves);
10. Attitudes of the parents.

For the parents, many hardships and stresses are associated with the disorder. To be informed, when expecting a normal healthy baby, that the child has a serious disabling condition is extremely stressful and usually results in feelings of helplessness and hopelessness. If prolonged, these feelings can lead to depression. Social workers should be aware of parental feelings and of the practical concerns that often arise in the care of a child with spina bifida. Parents need genetic information and answers to questions about the risk of having future children with the disorder. They need practical information on how to manage feeding problems, weight control, oral hygiene, skin care, bowel and urinary problems, and psycho-social issues. Some of the outside resources likely to be needed include: visiting nurses, infant stimulation programs, the Easter Seal program, respite care, special education, counseling programs, vocational guidance, special recreational programs, and, in some cases, financial aid.

### Case Study

Seth was almost 7 years of age when he was referred to the Sparks Center. His spina bifida was diagnosed at birth. The mother was shown the defect before it was surgically closed, and she remembered this as a "shocking sight" that left her frightened and depressed for weeks afterwards. She stated that she had no reason to suspect that the baby would have an abnormality, since her pregnancy had been unremarkable. The diagnosis of spina bifida was followed by months and years of surgery, illnesses, and other medical problems. There were several shunt revisions for hydrocephalus. Seth had seizures, a neurogenic bladder, esotropia, orthopedic problems, and generally delayed development.

The parents seemed to have made every effort to find the best available medical care for Seth. He was being followed not only by a local pediatrician and several State Crippled Children Services clinics but also by several specialists, including an ophthalmologist, a neurosurgeon, and an orthopedist. The family seemed to have spent a great deal of time in working with Seth at home and in implementing all medical recommendations.

Seth's enormous medical bills had been paid for by Blue Cross, since the father had a family plan insurance policy when Seth was born. Except for this, however, Seth was considered to be "uninsurable" because of his handicaps. Therefore, the family had not been able to obtain life or burial insurance on him other than at extremely "high-risk" rates which they chose not to pay. As an alternative to insurance, they had started a savings account in his name.

Seth was toilet trained, his eyes had been surgically straightened (he no longer wore glasses), and he was able to walk with the aid of braces, though he still walked with a bent knee, crouched gait. He slept and ate well and was reasonably independent in regard to taking care of his personal needs. He had a speech delay but did speak in short sentences. He received speech therapy at school. The mother admitted that he was "slow" in learning and estimated that he, at nearly 7 years of age, was functioning at the level of a 4- or 5-year-old. Both parents, however, tended to see this delay as a consequence of the early medical difficulties and the multiple surgeries, and both resisted vigorously the notion that any mental retardation per se was involved. (He attained a full-scale IQ of 63 on the WISC-R).

Now that Seth's medical situation was under control, the mother stated that her greatest concern was his need for an educational placement, along with planning for his future. These concerns had caused her great "heartbreak" and "frustration" because of trying to obtain services from school officials she believed had been unnecessarily uncooperative.

The social worker felt that the family had considerable strength and stability. They had certainly been strong advocates for their child, had sought the best medical care for him, and had diligently worked with him at home in many ways. With so many positive aspects to this family's situation, the social worker believed that the parents would deal eventually with one aspect of Seth's problems that they had not so far accepted (i.e. the fact that he was probably intellectually limited as well as physically handicapped). This fact was clearly and directly stated to the parents at the conference so that they could locate some type of educational placement for him. The social worker commented that "although hearing the diagnosis of mental retardation from outside professionals may be initially upsetting to the family, I believe that they will be able to cope with this in a constructive way, since they so obviously have Seth's ultimate good at heart."

Chapter Seven

# DISORDERS DUE TO OTHER CAUSES

## INFECTIONS (PRENATAL)

THIS CHAPTER reviews one disorder caused by an infection, congenital cytomegalovirus infection, and one disorder due to an endocrine dysfunction, congenital hypothyroidism. Seven disorders of unknown etiology are discussed, including Cornelia de Lange, Noonan, Prader-Willi, Rubinstein-Taybi, and Williams syndromes along with hydranencephaly and hydrocephalus.

### Congenital Cytomegalovirus Infection

Cytomegalovirus (CMV), a member of the herpes virus family, is one of the most common causes of congenital viral infections. This virus usually produces almost no symptoms in adults and older children, but, when it occurs during pregnancy, it can kill the unborn infant or cause birth defects. Some affected newborns are healthy and normal and are referred to as asymptomatic. Almost 1 percent of all live births have CMV; about 5 percent to 10 percent of these are symptomatic. How CMV causes birth defects is not known. (Friedman, 1981; Hanshaw, 1964; Stagno et al., 1982)

*Etiology*

The virus can be transmitted from the mother to the fetus in utero, from cervical secretions during the birth process or can be acquired through breast milk.

*Diagnosis*

Laboratory testing for CMV in body fluids is the most sensitive and specific method of diagnosis.

## Signs and Symptoms

The clinical signs are: microcephaly, seizures, motor disorders, central nervous system disorders, deafness, jaundice, enlarged liver and spleen, petechial rash (small purplish spots on the skin), and mental retardation. Hearing impairment varies from mild to profound. Speech and language impairments are commensurate with the degree of hearing loss and/or mental retardation. Patients sometimes show a yellowish discoloration of the teeth and have rampant dental caries. From 90 percent to 95 percent of infants with CMV who are symptomatic at birth will go on to develop one or more of these handicaps.

## Mental Retardation

Mental retardation varies from mild to profound; approximately 80 percent of the symptomatic children have some degree of retardation.

## Treatment Concerns

There is no effective medical treatment available for this disorder. Frequent audiological evaluations to monitor for progressive hearing impairment are indicated. Some patients will need hearing aids. Also, vision should be appropriately evaluated and, if necessary, followed for services to meet the child's visual needs. Treatment plans for the severely retarded should consist of a program that addresses the child's speech/language, cognitive, and self-help skills. Providing emotional support and information to the family is an essential part of the treatment plan. Because of the multiplicity of problems associated with the disorder, evaluation and treatment are best facilitated in an interdisciplinary setting.

## Case Study

Brian, age 16 months, was referred to the Sparks Center for evaluation of "delayed development subsequent to hospitalization for cytomegalovirus" (CMV) which was diagnosed at age 4 months. He was an only child living with his natural parents, both of whom were employed. The father worked as a clerk for a chemical company; the mother worked nights as a cashier for a restaurant. Since the father worked regular daytime hours and the mother worked at nights, Brian was always in the care of one of his parents. He never stayed with a babysitter and there were no relatives in the area, so the parents seldom got any respite from child care.

The social worker reported that the parents had a rather hectic life-style in which they passed each other as they went to and from their respective jobs. They expressed strong feelings about taking care of Brian themselves and had reservations about "sending him out" to a stimulation program or day-care facility "while he is still so young." They expressed much interest in having a home program of activities for him. They tended to talk about him in very hopeful terms, and the social worker speculated whether they really understood the reality of the situation. Both declared that they had no plans for additional children because they were having much difficulty, both financially and emotionally, in dealing with Brian.

The medical history indicated that Brian was a healthy baby until the age of 3 ½ months when he was hospitalized with the abrupt onset of pneumonitis (inflammation of the lung). This was believed to be related to CMV. Hospitalization lasted for three days. Following this, he was extremely lethargic and remained so until nearly 8 months of age. The results of the evaluations at the Sparks Center showed that he was functioning developmentally at about 10 months behind his chronological age of 16 months; speech was noted to be significantly delayed; he was having difficulty chewing and swallowing food; and he had trouble with his balance. Also, he appeared to have vision and hearing problems. However, it was questionable whether CMV per se could be considered as the sole or primary cause of his difficulties.

Nevertheless, staff consensus was that significant delays could be expected and that he would require special care and schooling for a long time. In view of the parents' reluctance to place Brian in an out-of-the-home program right away, it was decided that nursing, social work, and physical therapy would start with the family on a home program. The family needed information on appropriate special preschool programs in their area. Also, physical therapy intervention was indicated fairly soon because the parents were putting a lot of emphasis on his "walking." Staff recommended that Brian be seen by both speech/hearing and vision function, but social work continued to follow and coordinate services in the local area.

## METABOLISM AND NUTRITION

The American Association on Mental Deficiency's classification system includes in the "Metabolism or Nutrition" category many of the disorders caused by metabolic, nutritional, endocrine or growth dysfunction. Some of these disorders are discussed in other sections of this book. Selected for discussion here is congenital hypothyroidism, an endocrine disorder.

### Congenital Hypothyroidism (Athyrotic Hypothyroidism)

Congenital hypothyroidism is one of the most common endocrine disorders and occurs approximately one in every 6,000 births. It is a developmental defect in which there is partial or complete absence of the thyroid gland, or, in some cases, the gland is present but there is a defect in the release of the thyroid hormone. A deficiency of thyroid hormone can result in growth and developmental retardation. The term "cretinism" often is used synonymously with congenital hypothyroidism; however, the term should be avoided. (Menkes, 1985; Ziai, 1984)

### *Etiology*

Little is known as to the factors which interfere with the normal migration and development of the thyroid gland. The cause may be sporadic or familial; radioiodine administered during pregnancy can damage or wipe out the fetal thyroid.

### *Diagnosis*

The diagnosis is confirmed by laboratory analysis of TSH (thyroid-stimulating hormone, also known as thyrotropin). A newborn screening test for this disorder was developed in 1975. Prenatal diagnosis is not currently available.

### *Signs and Symptoms*

Clinical features of hypothyroidism usually are not present at birth but may begin to appear during the first week of life. Manifestations of hypothyroidism which appear in untreated children are: round, puffy, dull, expressionless face; enlarged anterior fontanelle; widely spaced eyes; narrow palpebral fissures; swollen eyelids; depressed nasal bridge; thick, broad tongue; hypotonicity; protruding abdomen; and herniated umbilicus. Other signs which may occur are: feeding problems, delayed dentition, slow speech, signs of vocal cord weakness, and varying degrees of mental retardation.

### *Mental Retardation*

If untreated, the result is neurological damage and mental deficiency.

## Treatment Concerns

Early diagnosis is important, and treatment should begin as soon after birth as possible to minimize irreversible brain damage. Treatment involves replacement therapy of the thyroid hormone and should continue for life. Treatment results in linear growth, osseous maturation, and sexual development. The effect on mental development is much less predictable, but the prognosis for mental development is poorer if the deprivation of thyroid hormone is more profound in the early months of life. Preliminary results indicate that treatment before age 6 weeks usually results in normal intelligence. Untreated, the condition will result in severe growth and mental retardation and can be fatal.

## Case Study

Marsha, who has congenital hypothyroidism, was 26 months old when a pediatric neurologist referred her for an interdisciplinary evaluation at the Sparks Center. During early pregnancy, the mother received radioiodine therapy for treatment of Graves disease. She was not aware of her pregnancy until the sixth month, at which time she was told of the possible effects that the medication could have on the baby. Marsha was delivered spontaneously at 7 ½ month gestation without complications. Birthweight was 3 pounds 3 ½ ounces. Thyroid therapy was begun shortly after birth for the disorder. Her general health has remained stable and she was being followed by an endocrinologist. The parents were concerned about her open fontanelle, umbilical hernia, diarrhea, and bald patches on her head. Sometimes it appeared that Marsha could not see. Also, her left foot appeared to turn inward. Marsha was experiencing significant delays; language and motor development have been the most noticeable areas of delay. She was not walking or talking.

Of great concern to the parents was the recent onset of Marsha's screaming while sleeping. They described her as a "mean" and "demanding" child who tended to control her older sister. The mother felt that Marsha was treated as a special child by both her father and the extended family. The father did assume a very active role in the caretaking of Marsha. Overall, however, the parents appeared to have had a very limited understanding of Marsha's condition and the prognosis.

From the evaluations it was found that Marsha, who was then 26 months of age, had the height of a 6-month-old and the weight of a 12-month-old child. Language skills were assessed at the 12-month level, motor skills between 17 and 20 months. Cognitively, she worked well at about 16 months. Physical findings included an umbilical hernia that required close observation and probable surgery at some point. She had a protruding abdomen, bow-shaped legs with flat feet, and an eye-hand coordination problem. Her eyes were widely set.

The recommendations were: (1) placement in a preschool program, (2) a home program designed to increase physical activity, (3) primary medical care to be provided by her private pediatrician who could follow her for other physical problems, and (4) application for SSI and Medicaid.

## UNKNOWN PRENATAL INFLUENCES

The etiology of many syndromes is known; however, the cause remains uncertain with others. This section reviews seven disorders for which no definite etiology can be established.

### Cornelia de Lange Syndrome

The major features of Cornelia de Lange syndrome are: (a) characteristic facies, (b) growth deficiency, (c) anomalies of the extremities, and (d) mental retardation. Some of the early symptoms are failure to cry normally at birth, weak sucking reflexes and difficult feeding. (Smith, 1982)

#### *Etiology*

The exact cause of the disorder is unknown; however, a genetic component probably is involved.

#### *Diagnosis*

The diagnosis is based on the clinical findings.

#### *Signs and Symptoms*

The typical facies of Cornelia de Lange syndrome include: long eyelashes; busy confluent eyebrows; hair growing down the forehead; thin lips; downward-curving angle of the mouth (carp mouth); smallness of the lower jaw (micrognathia); and small, round head (microbrachycephaly). The eyes are frequently widely spaced and slant downward, the nose is small and turns upward, and the nasal bridge is flat. Low-set ears is another characteristic, and abnormal hairiness (hirsutism) and hair whirls are common. Short stature at prenatal onset has been reported in all cases. Anomalies of the feet and hands frequently include the fusion of two or more toes or fingers (syndactyly), curvature of the small finger (clinodactyly), and small hands. With males, small genitalia and undescended testicles are common.

## Mental Retardation

Severe mental retardation has been reported in most all cases.

## Treatment Concerns

During infancy, episodes of aspiration and susceptibility to infections constitute the major health hazards. The overall conditions of the disorder reflect the need for a combination and a sequence of special interdisciplinary care which are of lifelong duration. These should be individually planned and coordinated and should include early intervention with a focus on language, motor, and self-help skills. Institutionalization may be an issue, and close supervision of the patient can be expected.

## Case Study

Jeremy weighed 4 pounds 8 ounces at birth. He had confluent eyebrows, upward-turned nose, and a peculiar hairline. Medical genetics found a normal karyotype, but they noted hirsutism, long curly eyelashes, and a thin upper lip. They requested to see Jeremy again to establish a diagnosis, but the family did not comply. All developmental milestones were delayed significantly.

At age 3, Jeremy was referred by the State Crippled Children Service to the Sparks Center. Findings were consistent with the diagnosis of Cornelia de Lange syndrome. His IQ was below 50, and he was also below the 5th percentile for height, weight, and head circumference. Evidence of a slight hearing loss was present, and he only spoke two or three words. His left foot was pronated, and he had a stiff gait. A structured preschool program with speech therapy was recommended.

Jeremy's parents, both in their mid-twenties, were separated after 7 years of marriage. They had been separated four times and the mother was hopeful that they could resolve matters as they had in the past.

The mother lived with her parents. The household consisted of Jeremy, his mother, two brothers, and a 6-month-old sister, as well as the maternal grandparents and a 17-year-old aunt. Source of income was ADC, but the family did not qualify for food stamps.

The diagnosis never had been discussed with the mother. She had failed to keep the 6-month follow-up appointment with medical genetics. Her main concern was with Jeremy's small size and his self-stimulating behavior. The mother reported that he masturbated, sucked two of his fingers, and continually played with his hair. She punished him for masturbating but had not noticed any change in this behavior.

At the parent conference, the mother was upset when told of the diagnosis, although she had suspected that something seriously was wrong all along. It was recommended that Jeremy be enrolled in a preschool program, but the mother had been denied enrollment in the past because Jeremy was not toilet trained. The mother returned to the center for a series of counseling sessions for her to learn more about the de Lange syndrome in general and to deal with the consequences of the disorder.

## Noonan Syndrome

Noonan syndrome affects both males and females. The syndrome in males is superficially similar to the Turner syndrome in females, but the general differences between the two syndromes are clinically evident. Also, mental retardation is more common with Noonan syndrome than with the Turner syndrome. The incident of the disorder may be as high as one in 1,000. (Batshaw & Perret, 1981; Ziai, 1984)

### Etiology

The cause of the disorder is unknown. However, many family histories of affected individuals suggest an autosomal dominant type of inheritance.

### Diagnosis

The diagnosis is based on the clinical findings, but the Noonan syndrome should be distinguished from the Turner syndrome. A normal karyotype in females rules out the Turner syndrome.

### Signs and Symptoms

The more common features of the disorder are: mental retardation; short stature; congenital heart disease; depressed sternum (pectus excavatum); webbing of the neck and characteristic facies (e.g. epicanthal eye folds); drooping eyelids; widely set eyes (hypertelorism); broad nasal bridge; and small chin. Males frequently have cryptorchidism (undescended testicles). Puffiness (lymphedema) on the back of the hands and feet are present at birth but may disappear as the patient gets older. Occasionally, vision or hearing problems are present; dental anomalies are common.

### Mental Retardation

Mental retardation is thought to occur in about 50 percent to 60 percent of the patients, though the degree of mental retardation seldom is severe.

### Treatment Concerns

Aside from the possibility of congenital heart disease, no apparent medical problems are unique to the Noonan syndrome. However, when mental retardation is present, special consideration should be given to educational planning. Adjustment problems related to secondary sexual characteristics, especially for males, may require counseling or guidance. Evaluations of vision and hearing function are advised prior to the initiation of any treatment or educational placement. Questions about the genetics of the disorder must be clarified for the parents.

### Case Study

Jimmy was the product of a normal gestation and delivery. But because of transient hyperbilirubinemia (treated with phototherapy), he spent two extra days in the nursery. A cardiac murmur was noted in the neonatal period, as well as some unusual facial characteristics. The cardiac murmur was subsequently diagnosed as pulmonic stenosis but was causing no problems; therefore, no surgery was necessary.

Developmentally, he was showing some delays and at age 9 months he was diagnosed by a private pediatrician as having Noonan syndrome. Referral was made to the Sparks Center for a comprehensive evaluation to determine appropriate treatment strategies. On physical exam, he manifested many of the features of

Noonan syndrome, including low posterior hairline, the characteristic facial features, pulmonic stenosis, short stature, microcephaly, and undescended testicles. Gross motor and language delays were apparent. Intellectually, he was functioning in the mild range of mental retardation. The hearing results suggested eustachian tube dysfunction; pre-language skills were delayed 2 to 5 months. From the series of evaluations, the recommendations shown below were made.

1. Follow-up by his pediatrician concerning the undescended testicles;
2. Careful monitoring of height/weight and head circumference;
3. Possible ventilation tubes if otitis media persisted;
4. Audiological re-evaluation;
5. Psychological re-evaluation;
6. An early stimulation program to help develop self-help and language skills;
7. Genetic counseling for the parents;
8. Social work services to assist the parents in dealing with the diagnosis;

The social work interview found that the parents were in their late-twenties and both had professional degrees. The mother was interviewed; the father avoided anything connected with the disorder and even questioned the validity of the diagnosis. Upon learning of the diagnosis, the mother began to read everything she could find about Noonan syndrome and searched the family background for any clues that other family members might have, or might have had, the disorder. She emphasized that no family members were ever retarded, but a male relative had several symptoms of the disorder.

Extended family members, especially Jimmy's grandmother, refused to discuss the matter and seemed ashamed that any family member might be retarded. When the grandmother learned of Jimmy's diagnosis, she became angry and discouraged any further reading on the subject with an attitude of "what you don't know won't hurt." Fortunately, Jimmy's mother did not share this attitude, and as a result of her interest, he received the recommended services over a period of time. Eventually, the father accepted the diagnosis, but the denial persisted on the part of other family members.

### Prader-Willi Syndrome

Prader-Willi syndrome is a disorder which seems to occur more often in males than females, possibly because it is more easily recognized in males.

The primary characteristics of the disorder are: obesity, poor muscle tone, mental retardation, and hypogonadism (decrease in the functioning of the testes and ovaries). Many patients develop diabetes mellitus during adult life. An excessive appetite with bizarre eating habits is associated with the disorder. (Hall & Smith, 1972; Pipes, 1978; Smith, 1982)

## Etiology

The etiology is unknown, but the pattern of characteristics associated with the disorder is remarkably consistent from patient to patient. Abnormal chromosome findings are reported in some cases.

## Diagnosis

The diagnosis is based on the clinical findings.

## Signs and Symptoms

The mean birthweight of affected individuals is several hundred grams less than the average birthweight of term babies. Hypotonia is most severe in early infancy. Tube feeding may be necessary because sucking and swallowing reflexes are poorly developed. After weeks or months, patients enter into a second clinical phase in which they become more responsive, and as feeding difficulties subside they become hungry and cry for food. Many then develop a voracious appetite and are capable of eating anything from pet food to garbage. As a consequence of their biazarre eating habits, they become extremely obese. The hands and feet usually remain disproportionately small. Height is usually below the 50th percentile. There is a delay of secondary sexual development. Undescended testes (cryptorchidism), small penis, and underdeveloped scrotum are evident among males. Small teeth with dental caries and enamel defects are common. A high arched palate may be found in some patients. Poorly formed ears and narrow external ear canals are occasionally encountered. The eyes are sometimes almond shaped with an upward slant.

## Mental Retardation

The level of intelligence of individuals with Prader-Willi syndrome varies from severe mental retardation to near normal. Most are mildly retarded or in the borderline category.

## Treatment Concerns

Controlling food intake and behavior are the most difficult aspects of the treatment plan. Behavioral problems, especially as they relate to food, make the management of obesity very difficult. Compounding the problem is the fact that patients usually seem to require considerably fewer calories to gain weight than the average person. Behavior management for the patient and counseling with the parents sometimes are effective treatment approaches; however, other problems related to the patient's health status, including dental health, should not be ignored. The obesity may result in peer rejection and ridicule, which may further complicate the treatment process. Special education for school-age patients can be expected. Vocational training in later years may be necessary for successful employment. Nevertheless, successful treatment requires careful planning and persistent attention from a variety of disciplines over a long period of time.

## Case Study

Bonnie was first referred to the center in 1965 when she was 5 years of age. Presenting problems were related to general developmental delays, obesity, and the need for help with future school planning. The developmental history revealed that she weighed 5 pounds 6 ounces at birth, was very weak with poor muscle tone, and required oxygen. For several weeks she did not cry or move, and it appeared that her muscle system would never achieve sufficient tone to carry on normal activities. She had considerable difficulty chewing and swallowing and was tube-fed for the first 3 months. Her weight was below the 5th percentile until she reached 24 months of age, at which time there was a dramatic increase in weight; it continued to increase over time. At the time of referral, she was well above the 95th percentile for weight. All developmental milestones were significantly delayed.

After a series of evaluations at the center, she was found to be mildly retarded, with speech, dental, motor and behavioral problems. The presence of certain physical features such as hypotonia, obesity, microcephaly, poorly shaped ears, high arched palate and small chin, along with the earlier clinical history and mental retardation, led to the diagnosis of Prader-Willi syndrome.

She was immediately placed on a diet and exercise program which was monitored over a period of time by the division of nutrition. During this time, social work provided weekly counseling sessions for the parents, who were experiencing a variety of problems. Particular attention was directed to helping them understand and accept the diagnosis and its consequences. Behavioral problems were a constant source of conflict. Being teased and ridiculed by her peers, and by a teenage brother who seemed to resent her, undoubtedly contributed to the behavioral problems. The weight-reduction program was not effective; occasionally, she lost weight but only after exteme efforts by all involved. The parents seemed to be emotionally drained in their attempts to control her behavior. She persistently stole petty items and presented immature, childish behavior with temper outbursts and an insatiable appetite.

An EMR placement was provided throughout her school career until she returned to the center for full-time vocational rehabilitation services at age 17. Her weight had reached 264 pounds; height was 5 feet. Throughout the placement, she continually stole food from the cafeteria, including cooked, uncooked and frozen foods. She also stole food from fellow students or anyone else who had food. Academically, she made some progress. However, weight loss was not accomplished, nor were the behavioral problems satisfactorily resolved. The parents, both of whom had serious health problems, were simply unable to follow through with any recommendation. The mother died from a long-standing health problem, and the father was unable to manage alone with Bonnie. She was placed in a group home through the regional mental health program.

## Rubinstein-Taybi Syndrome

Rubinstein-Taybi syndrome is a disorder involving mental retardation, broad thumbs and toes, and a characteristic facial appearance consisting of a "beaked" nose, small head (microcephaly), prominent forehead, and small lower jaw (micrognathia). The incidence of the disorder in the general population is unknown. In the mentally retarded population, the frequency has ranged from one in 300 to one in 700 individuals. (Gellis et al., 1968; Rubinstein & Taybi, 1963)

### Etiology

The etiology is unknown.

### Diagnosis

The diagnosis is based on the clinical findings.

### Signs and Symptoms

During the neonatal period, major medical difficulties are reported to occur (e.g. recurrent respiratory infections, feeding difficulties, and various allergic states). Broad thumbs and toes have been present in all reported cases. The fifth finger may curve inward (clinodactyly). Facial characteristics include a small head (microcephaly), broad nasal bridge, beaked nose, and an underdeveloped lower jaw (micrognathia). The mouth has a high arched palate. Occasional features of the eyes are: widely set eyes (hypertelorism), squint (strabismus), and drooping eyelids (ptosis).

Growth retardation and delayed bone age typify the disorder. Some of the skeletal anomalies include a depressed sternum (pectus excavatum), curvature of the spine (scoliosis), anterior curvature of the spine (lordosis), and posterior curvature of the spine (kyphosis). Due to lax ligaments, hyperextensibility of the joints is likely; loss of muscle tone (hypotonia) is almost always present. Most males have undescended testes (cryptorchidism) and many have urinary tract anomalies.

### Mental Retardation

The level of mental retardation for Rubinstein-Taybi syndrome is usually below 50.

### Treatment Concerns

Special education, probably in a trainable class, is usually required. Institutionalization may be the best means of care for the profoundly handicapped. Speech therapy for problems associated with overall delays and with palatal imperfections can be expected. The high incidence of other defects of the mouth undoubtedly will require frequent dental attention. Medical care from a variety of specialists can be anticipated including neurology for possible seizure activity, ophthalmology for visual defects, orthopedics for skeletal anomalies, and urology for urinary tract problems. The multi-handicapping features associated with the disorder, which often are severe or profound, call for a comprehensive treatment plan with interdisciplinary support that ideally takes into consideration the emotional and social needs of the entire family.

### Case Study

Phillip, at age 5 years 2 months, was referred to the Sparks Center by a nurse at the State Crippled Children Service. Although he was already diagnosed as having Rubinstein syndrome, the referral source indicated that not everyone was in agreement with the diagnosis. Phillip was seen in clinic in June 1983 and was accompanied by his mother, stepfather, grandmother, two aunts, and an uncle. The mother was not certain as to why the child was referred, nor did she express any particular concerns. She did not appear to be seeking diagnostic information or an evaluation of developmental status.

During the interview with the social worker, the mother mentioned that Phillip had been seen by medical genetics in the past. Records were then obtained from medical genetics, indicating that Phillip had been seen on two occasions, at age 5 months and again at age 1 year. He had been diagnosed as having Rubinstein-Taybi syndrome. Findings supporting the diagnosis included short and broad thumbs and great toes, fourth digit on each foot overlapping the third, microcephaly, triangular-shaped head, and high narrow palate. The parents were counselled with regard to the diagnosis, but the mother did not demonstrate adequate understanding of Phillip's condition. Her recall of the counseling session included only the facts that Phillip would have respiratory problems and would be slow. She believed that he had made more progress than was initially anticipated.

Phillip's mother was only 14 years of age when he was born; on the clinic date, she was 19 years old and divorced from Phillip's natural father. She had recently remarried and was in the first trimester of her second pregnancy. The stepfather, age 19, was unemployed aside from an occasional job as a farmhand. This low socioeconomic family lived with the paternal grandmother's family and did not plan to establish an independent household in the near future. Consistent income was limited to supplemental security income (SSI) received for Phillip. The mother had a paternal aunt, who was handicapped.

Phillip was attending a school for the handicapped in his home town, but the mother was not sure what services he was receiving. Phillip did not present any particular problems to the mother, nor did she express any major concerns about him. She seemed to understand that Phillip was and will continue to be slow but did not speculate (when asked) as to why this might be. She indicated she had been told very little about Phillip's prior evaluations at State Crippled Children Service. She did not express any desire to know more about these evaluations, nor did she express any dissatisfaction about the services received in the past. Nevertheless, the social work staff encouraged her to contact medical genetics again about her current pregnancy (the medical genetics report noted a 1% risk in such cases). Also, the social worker contacted the staff at State Crippled Children Service to make sure that the center's recommendations—school placement, testing by medical genetics, and other types of services—were available and coordinated.

## Williams Syndrome

Williams syndrome is characterized by unusual facies, mental retardation, growth deficiency, cardiovascular anomalies (variable finding), and occasionally hypercalcemia. The syndrome is sometimes referred to as "elfin facies" syndrome and idiopathic hypercalcemia-supravalvular aortic stenosis syndrome. The incidence of the syndrome is reported to be rare. (Gorlin et al., 1976; Smith, 1982)

### *Etiology*

The etiology is unknown; all reported cases have been sporadic.

### *Diagnosis*

The diagnosis is based on the clinical findings. In some cases, hypercalcemia may be present during the first few years following birth.

### *Signs and Symptoms*

The major features of the disorder are: peculiar facies, flat mid face, depressed nasal bridge, anteverted small nose, broad upper jaw, small lower jaw, full prominent upper lip (cupid's bow), increased surface of upper lip (philtrum), full cheeks, open mouth, medial eyebrow flaring, widely set eyes (hypertelorism), epicanthal folds, high percentage of blue-eyed individuals with stellate iris pattern, high arched palate, possibly small teeth (microdontia), cardiovascular anomalies, and short stature.

### *Mental Retardation*

The level of mental retardation is moderate to borderline.

### *Treatment Concerns*

When hypercalcemia is still present, it is necessary to eliminate vitamin D from the diet and to limit the intake of calcium. Feeding problems may require special attention during infancy. Special education, based on intellectual functioning, should be anticipated. Occasionally, severe behavioral problems are reported to be a treatment issue, but most patients are reported to be outgoing and loquacious, especially during childhood.

### Case Study

Chris, at age 9, came to the attention of the Sparks Center through the State Crippled Children Service. The referring social worker did not mention multiple or complex problems but was mainly concerned about academic and coordination problems. However, clinical findings at the center suggested a diagnosis of Williams syndrome. He was found to be borderline mentally retarded and had many of the features of Williams syndrome, including growth deficiency, characteristic facial features, the stellate pattern in the iris, cryptorchidism, and behavioral problems. He still had a heart problem ("leaky valve"), despite previous cardiac surgery. The possibility existed that he might require further heart surgery and he was supposed to see a pediatric cardiologist once a year. Additional medical problems were: hypospadias, enuresis, chronic ear infection, an esotropia, frequent eye irritations, and "flat feet." Also, after a previous clinic visit, dental treatment had been strongly recommended because of caries and periodontal disease, which had progressed to a more serious state.

The parents' main concerns were (1) poor school achievement, (2) his poor coordination, (3) his chronic medical problems, and (4) his atypical behavior, especially his tendency towards cruelty and destructiveness.

Chris was reported to be distractible with a short attention span. Beyond this, the parents expressed pronounced concern over several episodes of cruel behavior exhibited by Chris (i.e. nearly causing serious injury to an infant cousin by trying to pull him through the slatted side of a crib). It bothered the parents that when Chris openly discussed what he had done, he showed no remorse and seemed unaware of the seriousness of his acts. He had few friends, kept to himself and sat "daydreaming" quite a bit. Sometimes he made odd, out-of-context remarks that did not make sense. He was repeating the second year of school with very little progress being shown.

Chris was from a low-income family of five living in a rural county. The father, a construction worker, had only sporadic employment over the past two years, partly because of frequent layoffs and partly because he had suffered a painful back injury on the job. The mother worked part-time to help supplement the lost income. They had no medical insurance and were on no benefit programs except that the children received free lunches. Most of the medical care for Chris had been provided by the State Crippled Children Service.

One of the social work interviews several months after the initial clinic visit yielded significant information. The mother revealed one day that she, her two oldest sons and numerous relatives of hers, both male and female, all were losing their sight due to retinitis pigmentosa which is a heritable genetic disease. The mother stated, quite casually, that she was already blind in one eye and had only very constricted sight in the other. She expected to be blind by age 40 and was told that she could no longer drive because of the hazards involved. She continued to drive, however, because her livelihood demanded it. The two sons did not present severe symptoms and still were able to attend regular classes.

The acceptance that three members of the immediate family were losing their sight was remarkable. The mother seemed to feel that blindness was just something, like blond hair, or blue eyes, that runs in the family and that since nothing can be done about it, there was no point in being upset about it. Obviously, the mother and children have had no genetic counseling, nor had there been any realistic planning for how the family would function when the mother/wife must adjust to a lack of sight. Neither had the family given serious thought as to how Chris's special needs would be met by a non-sighted, primary-care giver. Referral was made to a deaf/blind program and to the genetics laboratory at the medical center. Total family counseling was also recommended to deal with a number of issues.

According to the social worker, these parents appeared to be concerned, caring people, who, perhaps because of a lack of sophistication and other factors, had a very low-key, non-interventionist approach to their very considerable difficulties. A chronic lack of money and reliable transportation, no doubt, have exacerbated their tendency to "do nothing" about resolving their problems, and they certainly did not see the possibilities regarding what improvements realistically might be made. In view of these factors, the family had shown evidence of being survivors. Considering that all five members of this family have serious and, to different degrees, disabling health problems, and that they function in a low-income, rural environment with few resources of any sort, they were to be commended for maintaining any semblance of a normal life-style.

## Hydranencephaly

Hydranencephaly is a congenital malformation in which the cerebral hemispheres either are missing or have huge defects. The skull and scalp are formed normally. The cerebral hemispheres are replaced by a large fluid-filled cavity. The incidence of the disorder is rare. (Ford, 1966; Gellis et al., 1968; Menkes, 1985)

### Etiology

The etiology of this condition is unknown. It is not, however, an inherited disorder.

### Diagnosis

The diagnosis is suspected by total transillumination of the skull. Also, a CAT scan should differentiate this condition from other similar disorders. The EEG shows little or no electrical activity. Angiograms show very thin rudimentary cerebral arteries.

### Signs and Symptoms

Infants with this disorder usually appear normal at birth. However, after a few weeks it may become evident that the child is not developing normally. The infant is often irritable and cries and/or screams excessively. Normal voluntary movements are not evident; generalized or minor seizures may occur; and incoordinated eye movements are apparent. Other features of the disorder include hyperreflexia, hypertonia, and quadriparesis. The life span for the majority of these patients is only a few weeks or months. However, a few cases have been documented in which patients with the disorder survived several years.

### Mental Retardation

Affected individuals are severely to profoundly retarded.

### Treatment Concerns

In most cases, no effective treatment of the condition is available. For patients who survive past the first few months of life, an early intervention program is suggested. Ideally, such a program should provide interdisciplinary care from a variety of disciplines (e.g. nursing, social work, physical therapy, nutrition, medicine, and others as indicated). In such a program, particular attention should be directed to neurodevelopmental stimulation.

Parents of these youngsters will need considerable support and training to help them deal with the emotional impact that the disorder has on the entire family, and to assist them in providing nurturance in the home. Ideally, the counseling/educational process is best provided by an interdisciplinary team in conjunction with an early intervention program. This allows the parents to observe as well as participate in the treatment process.

### Case Study

Nicole was born by C-section four weeks postmature, and hydranencephaly was diagnosed during the perinatal period. This was the first child born to a 21-year-old mother and a 23-year-old father who was in his last year of college as a business major. Both parents seemed to handle the diagnosis very well; however, as time passed, the day-to-day care of Nicole demanded much of their time, especially the mother's, and she was left physically and emotionally exhausted. At 20 days, it was determined that Nicole needed shunting, and physicians inserted a ventriculo-peritoneal (V-P) shunt. She tolerated the procedure well. According to the parents, they had been told that Nicole would die within the first 6 months and this added to their anxieties. (She was 3 years of age on their last clinic visit.)

When Nicole was 5 months of age, she was referred to the Sparks center's infant stimulation program which she and her mother both attended for about two years. The nature of her disorder required consistent and continuing care by an interdisciplinary team of child-care specialists, and in this process social work provided supportive counseling to the mother. Through physical therapy, attempts were made to prevent abnormal posturing and contractures. Also, Nicole needed much direct care and handling. She did not have any vision, and feeding problems were also present. She had been eating table food until about age 3, at which time she became irritable with crying spells and refused food. In addition, Nicole was having three or four seizures each day, as well as one or two at night which were causing the mother to lose a lot of sleep.

Because it is unlikely that Nicole will ever develop independent functioning, as she grows older she will continue to require increased involvement from both parents. This situation was extremely difficult and stressful for the mother, who had to assume almost total parenting responsibilities because the father had a job which required him to travel frequently. Nicole eventually was referred to a community-based program.

### Hydrocephalus

Hydrocephalus is a disorder in which the cerebral ventricular system is dilated and contains excessive amounts of cerebral spinal fluid. Hydrocephaly also may accompany a number of other birth defects (e.g. spina bifida). The incidence of the disorder is approximately 0.8 to 1.6 cases per 1,000 children. (Apgar & Beck, 1974; Ford, 1966; Wolraich, 1983)

### *Etiology*

An increase in intraventricular pressure occurs as a result of obstruction to the flow of cerebral spinal fluid. The result of this obstruction is the buildup of fluid; if untreated, this condition causes pressure on the brain, leading to brain damage.

One type of hydrocephalus is inherited (X-linked recessive), and the chances of its recurrence in that particular family can be predicted. Some hydrocephalus has no hereditary basis, and other types are thought to be the result of a combination of genetic and prenatal factors.

### *Diagnosis*

If an infant has an unusually large head or if there is evidence of a faster-than-normal increase in head size, hydrocephalus should be suspected. A CAT scan is often helpful in confirming the diagnosis. Additional diagnostic procedures can include encephalography, pneumoencephalography, ventriculography, or arteriography.

### *Signs and Symptoms*

The enlarged head is the most striking feature of the disorder. The face appears relatively small, and the ears may be low set with possible hearing deficits. There may be paralysis of the upper or lower extremities. Additionally, various types of skeletal deformities have been associated with the disorder. In advanced untreated cases, the eyes have a downward look so that the white area above the pupil is prominent; this is called the "setting sun" appearance. Seizures frequently are associated with hydrocephalus. Some patients are irritable and restless, while others may be abnormally quiet. They may be nauseated or may present feeding problems as a result of increased intracranial pressure. In severe cases, the child may die *in utero*.

### Mental Retardation

For patients who receive proper medical and neurological treatment, resulting in an arrest of the hydrocephalus, approximately 50 percent are expected to have normal intelligence, 25 percent are retarded but educable, and 25 percent are severely retarded.

### Treatment Concerns

In some cases, hydrocephalus becomes partially arrested; however, complete arrest of the disorder is probably very rare. When the disorder progressively worsens, treatment should begin as soon as possible. An artificial shunt is used most commonly to treat hydrocephalus. Often, problems are associated with the shunt, such as complications from infections which may require additional surgery. Children also can outgrow the shunt which is then replaced with longer tubing.

For the multiply impaired, a series of treatment programs should be anticipated. An evaluation to determine intellectual functioning is essential for proper educational placement. The orthopedically involved will need a program providing self-help training for ambulation, and toileting and feeding problems. Hearing deficits and visual impairment should be ruled out prior to the initiation of educational or habilitation programs.

It is helpful for parents to have access to a parent group. The education and training of parents to care for the disabled child in the home should be included in the treatment plan. Families also must have access to a variety of support systems, such as respite care, baby-sitting, and homemaker services, in order to help them cope with what might develop into an extremely demanding and stressful situation.

### Case Study

James was delivered by C-section after prolonged labor due to hydrocephalus (family history was positive for hydrocephalus; mother's sister had spina bifida but was not retarded). The hydrocephalus was diagnosed by an abdominal film. At birth, James's head circumference was 53 cm (34–35 cm is normal). He had respiratory distress and was transferred to a regional newborn intensive care unit. The first shunt was placed at 4 days of age and subsequently there was good decompression. Shortly thereafter, he developed a staphylococcal shunt infection requiring shunt removal and, one week later, replacement. About a year later, he was admitted for shunt malfunction and required two shunt revisions during that time. His symptoms of shunt malformation included persistent vomiting, veins on his scalp filling up, and his fontanelle becoming full. The mother stated that he also became irritable and fussy when such problems developed. Other health problems were otitis media and a constant nasal congestion. Apart from the disproportion of his head to body, he appeared healthy, alert and interactive. Developmentally, he seemed to be progressing fairly well, although he was showing some signs that might indicate developmental problems such as a failure to "reach."

James lived with his natural parents, both of whom were in their mid-twenties. The father was unemployed, and the family was receiving unemployment compensation which was to be discontinued. James was receiving SSI, Medicaid, and WIC; the family's rent was subsidized by HUD. There had been some speculation that the parents' expectations of James were unrealistic, primarily because they were comparing him to the 22-year-old aunt who had spina bifida and hydrocephalus. Because of the severity of hydrocephalus and complications with shunts, the parents were told by health professionals in their local area that he probably would not survive. The aunt, who was not shunted, was not expected to survive, either (this information represented the parents' interpretation). In comparing the situations, these parents seemed to have learned the importance of hope. While their expectations may not have been commensurate with what they had been told about the prognosis, they nevertheless were aware that James might have developmental problems.

Two sets of grandparents had taken opposing views of James. The maternal grandparents were supportive and believed that he would be normal, while the paternal grandparents were frightened of James and refused to hold him. However, in the immediate family, communication appeared to be good, and the social worker believed that the parents were making a remarkable adjustment to having a child with both a visible and serious condition. A referral was made to medical genetics in view of the family history. Also, James was referred for an early intervention program in his local community.

## Appendix

# SELECTED REVIEW OF ADDITIONAL
# MENTAL RETARDATION SYNDROMES

CROUZON SYNDROME: Autosomal dominant in many cases. There is a characteristic appearance of an abnormally misshapen head and face and widely set, bulging eyes. The midface may be underdeveloped. The lower jaw may be prominent compared to the upper jaw. Mental retardation may be mild to moderate; however, most have normal mental abilities.

FETAL ALCOHOL SYNDROME: Caused by chronic maternal alcoholism. Some features are small head (microcephaly), drooping eyelids (ptosis), squint eyes (strabismus), frequently a hairy face (hirsutism), and a variety of facial abnormalities. Mental retardation is generally mild, but some patients are reported to be at a lower level.

HURLER SYNDROME (MUCOPOLYSACCHARIDOSIS I, GARGOYLISM): Autosomal recessive inheritance. The disorder shows skeletal abnormalities, short stature, and coarse facial features. Also cardiac, respiratory, hearing and visual problems may be present. Onset appears to be by 1 to 2 years of age. Mental retardation is severe.

KERNICTERUS: Results from destruction of the fetal red blood cells *in utero* (usually Rh incompatibility). Severe motor and sensory problems may occur, but with treatment no one physical sign is characteristic of this disorder. Mental retardation varies from mild to severe, depending on the success of treatment.

LESCH-NYHAN SYNDROME: X-linked recessive inheritance. There is a tendency towards self-mutilation (lip biting, finger chewing, etc.), usually starting by the second year of life. Spasticity and athetoid movements may be present. Mental retardation is at the severe level.

SMITH-LEMLI-OPITZ SYNDROME: The disorder is thought to be caused by the autosomal recessive mode of inheritance. Features of the disorder include abnormal genital development, short stature, skeletal defects, and abnormalities of the head and hands. Mental retardation is from moderate to severe.

SOTOS CEREBRAL GIGANTISM: Etiology is unknown. The disorder shows excessively rapid growth during the first 4 to 5 years of life. The patient is tall with a large head, hands, and feet. Aggressive, irritable-type behaviors are sometimes present. Mental retardation is mild to moderate.

HOMOCYSTINURIA: Autosomal recessive (inborn error of amino acid metabolism). Patients sometimes exhibit features of Marfan syndrome. They may have elongated body, spider-like hands, fingers, pectus excavatum, and cardiac problems. Death is usually before age 30 in 25 percent of the patients. Mental retardation is common in untreated patients.

CRI DU CHAT (CAT CRY) SYNDROME: A congenital abnormality in which there is a partial deletion of the small arm of the number 5 chromosome. Patients have severe psychomotor retardation plus physical and neurological problems. A cat-like cry during infancy is a characteristic of the disorder. The mental retardation level is usually severe.

SANFILIPPO SYNDROME (MUCOPOLYSACCHARIDOSIS III): Possibly autosomal recessive mode of inheritance. Similar to Hunter and Hurler syndrome but not as devastating. Coarse facial features and skeletal deformities are common. Mental retardation usually develops at about 1–4 years of age.

TOXOPLASMOSIS: The disorder is caused by an infection (protozoan) during pregnancy. Some infected infants are born with defects (i.e. microcephaly, hydrocephalus, calcification in the brain, epilepsy, deafness, and eye damage). Mental retardation ranges from mild to severe.

LOWE SYNDROME: X-linked mode of inheritance. Affected individuals frequently have visual defects, bizarre behaviors, generalized motor retardation, and other physical anomalies. Mental retardation is usually at the severe level.

MICROCEPHALY: A head circumference less than two standard deviations below the mean suggests microcephaly. This condition is often seen (secondary microcephaly) with other syndromes or with other conditions (e.g. neonatal asphyxia, severe malnutrition, fetal alcohol syndrome). An X-linked type of microcephaly has been reported. Usually, primary microcephaly has an autosomal recessive etiology. Mental retardation generally ranges from moderate to profound with primary microcephaly.

MYOTONIC DYSTROPHY: Inherited as an autosomal dominant trait. Major features of this disorder are: tonic spasms of the muscles (mytonia), reduced muscle tension (hypotonia), endocrine disturbances, early feeding problems, drooping eyelids (ptosis), and mild to moderate mental retardation.

WILSON DISEASE: Autosomal recessive mode of inheritance. It is a rare inborn error of copper metabolism disease. Some characteristics of the disease are: drooling mouth, contracture of the wrist joint, and Kayser-Fleischer ring (greenish-brown pigment of the cornea of the eyes). Liver disease may be a problem. Mental retardation of varying degrees may not manifest itself until the school years or adulthood.

TRISOMY 18 (EDWARDS) SYNDROME: This disorder is due to nondisjunction in almost all cases. Some common features are: mental retardation, weak cry, hypertonicity, feeding problems, failure to thrive, and various other physical anomalies. The prognosis for children with this disorder is poor. Approximately 90 percent die by one year of age.

ANGLEMAN (HAPPY PUPPET) SYNDROME: The cause is undetermined. The disorder is characterized by sudden inappropriate laughter, ataxia, seizures, abnormal EEG, microcephaly, protruding tongue, and other facial anomalies. Severe to profound mental retardation is reported.

KLIPPEL-TRENAUNAY-WEBER SYNDROME (ANGIOOSTEOHYPERTROPHY): The etiology is unknown. Manifestations frequently include unilateral leg hypertrophy with cutaneous and subcutaneous hemangiomas. However, findings can include most all body areas (i.e. abnormalities of the fingers and toes and problems of the vascular system). Patients are at increased risk for mental retardation.

SAETHRE-CHOTZEN SYNDROME: The etiology is autosomal dominant. Some of the features of the disorder include premature closure of the sutures of the skull (craniosynostosis), facial asymmetry, beaked nose, drooping eyes (ptosis), low-set ears, anomalies of the hands, short stature, and various dental problems. Mild to moderate mental retardation has been observed, though most individuals are intellectually normal.

# GLOSSARY

**Acrocephaly**
A high or peaked appearance of the head.

**Adaptive behavior**
The degree to which an individual meets expected standards of personal independence and social responsibility when compared with age and social norms.

**Alleles**
Alternate form of a gene occupying the same locus on homologous chromosomes.

**Amniocentesis**
The withdrawal of amniotic fluid surrounding the fetus which can be studied chemically or cytologically to detect genetic disorders.

**Ankylosis**
A condition in which joints of the bones are fixed or fused.

**Anoxia**
Deficiency of oxygen.

**Aphasia**
The impairment of language function as a result of dysfunction of brain centers.

**Apraxia**
Inability to perform purposive movements; it is associated with central nervous system damage.

**Arachnodactyly**
Long, slender spider-like fingers or toes.

**Asphyxia**
Condition caused by insufficient intake of oxygen.

**Ataxia**
Incoordination of certain motor functions.

**Athetosis**
A condition, due to brain damage, in which there is involuntary movements of certain parts of the body (i.e. the extremities).

**Atonia**
Without normal muscle tone.

**Atrophy**
A wasting or decrease in size of an organ or tissue.

**Autosome**
All chromosomes (22 pairs) except sex chromosomes.

**Bilirubin**
A substance produced from the destruction of red blood cells.

**Brachycephaly**
Shortness of the head.

**Brachydactyly**
An abnormal shortness of the fingers or toes.

**Brushfield spots**
Gray or pale yellow spots of the iris, sometimes seen in children with Down syndrome.

**Cafe-au-lait spots**
Spots of patchy pigmentation of skin, usually light brown in color.

**Carrier**
One who carries a recessive gene together with its normal allele.

**Chorioretinitis**
An inflammation of the choroid and retina.

**Chromatography**
A method of separating two or more chemical compounds.

**Chromosome**
Carriers of genes and present in cell nucleus. They are divided in groups A–G (1–22). Sex chromosomes are not numbered. The normal number in humans is 46, with 22 pairs of autosomes and 2 sex chromosomes (XX or XY).

**Cleft palate**
A congenital defect in which there is a fissure formation in the roof of the mouth.

**Clinodactyly**
A congenital defect in which there is an abnormal deflection of the fingers or toes.

**Clubfoot**
A congenital defect of the foot.

**Coloboma**
A congenital fissure of the eye.

**Congenital**
Present at birth.

**Craniostenosis**
Refers to the premature closing or fusion of the cranial sutures.

**Cryptorchidism**
Undescended testes.

**Cytogenetics**
The study of the structure and function of chromosomes.

**Deletion**
Loss of part of a chromosome that results in an imbalance of genetic material.

**DNA (deoxyribonucleic acid)**
A nucleic acid found in all living cells.

**Dolichocephaly**
Pertains to a head that is significantly longer than it is broad.

**Dominant gene**
A gene which produces an effect regardless of its allele.

**Dysmorphism**
Abnormal development in the structure and form of an individual.

**Dysostosis**
A defect in the development of bone.

**Electroencephalogram (EEG)**
A graphic recording of the electrical activity of the brain.

**Encephalopathy**
Refers to brain disease.

**Enophthalmos**
Recession of eyeball into orbit.

**Epicanthal folds**
A fold of skin in the inner corner of the eye.

**Esotropia**
A form of strabismus in which the eye turns inward.

**Eugenics**
The study of methods to improve the herditary constitution of a species.

**Exotropia**
A form of strabismus in which the eye turns outward.

**Familial**
The appearance of a trait in several members of a sibship, family, or kindred.

**Fetoscopy**
A procedure that allows direct visualation of the fetus.

**Fibroma**
A benign tumor of fibrous connective tissue.

**Fissure**
A groove or narrow division in an organ of the body.

**Fontanelle**
A "soft spot" lying between the cranial bones of the skull of an infant.

**Gamete**
Mature gene cell (ovum or sperm) containing unpaired chromosomes.

**Gene**
A unit of heredity located on the chromosomes.

**Genotype**
The actual genetic makeup of an individual.

**Genu valgum**
Knock-knee.

**Gonadal dysgenesis**
Refers to the underdevelopment of the sex glands.

**Grand mal seizure**
A form of epileptic attack.

**Gynecomastia**
Large breasts in males.

**Hemangioma**
A benign tumor of dilated blood vessels.

**Hemiparesis**
Weakness of one side of the body.

**Hepatomegaly**
An increase in the size of the liver.

**Heterozygote**
An individual in whom two members of a pair of alleles are different (carriers).

**Hirsutism**
Excessive amount of hair on parts of the body.

**Homozygote**
An individual in whom two members of a pair of alleles are the same.

**Hyperbilirubinemia**
An abnormal amount of bilirubin levels in the blood.

**Hyperextensibility**
To be able to overextend a joint.

**Hyperplasia**
Excessive proliferation of normal cells in the tissue of an organ.

**Hypertelorism**
An excessive distance between two paired organs (i.e. the eyes).

**Hypertonia**
Increase in muscle tone.

**Hypertrichosis**
Growth of hair in excess of normal.

**Hypocalcemia**
A decrease in the calcium level in the blood.

**Hypogonadism**
Defective internal secretion of the gonads.

**Hypoplasia**
Defective development of tissue.

**Hypotrichosis**
Abnormal deficiency of hair.

**Hypoxia**
Deficiency of oxygen.

**Idiopathic**
Any condition in which the cause is unkown.

**Incontinent**
Inability to control bowel or bladder function.

**Inversion**
A reversal of the usual gene order along a segment of a chromosome.

**Karyotype**
The pictorial arrangement of matched pairs of chromosomes.

**Kyphoscoliosis**
An abnormal posterior and lateral curvature of the spine.

**Kyphosis**
An abnormal posterior curvature of the spine.

**Locus**
The position that a gene occupies on a chromosome.

**Lordosis**
An abnormal anterior curvature of parts of the spine.

**Lumbar**
The lower part of the back.

**Macrocephaly**
An abnormally large head.

**Macroglossia**
Large tongue.

**Macro-orchidism**
Large testicles.

**Malocclusion**
Imperfect closure of the teeth.

**Meiosis**
Process of all division which produces the ovum and sperm with unpaired chromosomes.

**Meninges**
Membrane coverings of the brain or spinal cord.

**Microcephaly**
Abnormally small head.

**Micrognathia**
Abnormally small jaw.

**Mitosis**
Normal cell division.

**Mosaicism**
At least two cell lines differing in genetic structures.

**Multifactorial**
A situation in which more than one factor is responsible for the appearance of a disorder. Thought to be a combination of genetic and environmental factors.

**Mutation**
A change in a gene resulting in permanent, transmissible change in the genetic makeup of an individual.

**Myoclonic seizures**
Intermittent spasms or twitching of a muscle or muscles.

**Myopathy**
Disease of muscle tissue

**Nodule**
A small node.

**Nondisjunction**
The failure of paired chromosomes to separate during meiosis or mitosis.

**Nystagmus**
A vertical or horizontal oscillatory movement of the eyeball.

**Occiput**
The back part of the skull.

**Ossification**
Process of bone formation.

**Palate**
Roof of the mouth.

**Paresis**
Weakness caused by loss of muscle power.

**Pectus carinatum**
Abnormal prominence of the sternum ("pigeon breast").

**Pectus excavatum**
Abnormally depressed sternum ("funnel breast").

**Pedigree**
Schematic presentation of a family tree.

**Penetrance**
The frequency of expression of a genotype is less than 100 percent.

**Pes excavatum**
Abnormally high-arched foot.

**Pes planus**
Flat foot.

**Petechiae**
Small round spots on the skin resulting from minute hemorrhage.

**Phenotype**
External appearance of an individual.

**Polydactyly**
An extra finger or toe.

**Proband or propositus**
The individual in question, usually the identified patient.

**Prognathia**
The lower jaw projects.

**Ptosis**
Drooping of the upper eyelid or of other body parts.

**Recessive**
A gene which has no effect in the presence of a dominant allele but does have an effect in the homozygous individual.

**Sclerosis**
Hardening of any part or tissue of the body.

**Scoliosis**
Abnormal lateral curvature of the spine.

**Sex chromosome**
Normal males have one X and Y (XY); normal females have two Xs (XX).

**Shunt**
The process of making an alternate pathway to reduce intracranial fluid pressure (i.e. hydrocephalus).

**Simian crease**
A single transverse crease on the palms of the hand as seen in some syndromes (e.g. Down syndrome).

**Spasticity**
An increase in muscle tone or tension.

**Stenosis**
Narrowing of an opening.

**Syndactyly**
Fingers or toes that are joined together as seen in Apert syndrome.

**Syndrome**
A number of birth defects which consistently occur together.

**Synophrys**
Confluent eyebrows as seen in Cornelia de Lange syndrome.

**Teratogen**
An agent (i.e. drugs) that is thought to cause birth defects.

**Toxoplasma**
A protozoan organism that causes a congenital infection of the fetus resulting in toxoplasmosis.

**Trachael malacia**
Soft tissue of the trachea.

**Trait**
Any genetically determined characteristic.

**Translocation**
The transfer of a part of a chromosome to another chromosome.

**Trisomy**
The presence of three particular chromosomes instead of the normal two.

**Ultrasound**
A technique of prenatal examination of the fetus and uterus by use of sound waves.

**Variable expressivity**
Refers to the wide range of phenotypes that can result in different individuals who have the same genotype.

**X-linked**
Trait carried on the X chromosome.

**Zygote**
The product of the union of ovum and sperm.

# REFERENCES AND
# SELECTED BIBLIOGRAPHY

Adoption Assistance and Child Welfare Act of 1980 (Public Law 96-272), 42 U.S.C. 1305, 94 STAT 500 et seq.

Alexander, H. et al. (1981). *Tomorrow's children: A special student report on mental retardation prevention.* Nashville: State of Tennessee, Governor's Task Force.

*\*AMA diagnostic and treatment guidelines concerning child abuse and neglect. (1985).* Report of Council on Scientific Affairs. *Journal of the American Medical Association, 254*(6), 796-800.

Anderson, E.M. & Spain, B. (1977). *The child with spina bifida.* London: Methuen.

Apgar, V. & Beck, J. (1974). *Is my baby all right?* New York: Trident Press.

Badger, E. (1977). The infant stimulation/mother training project. In B. Caldwell and D. Stedman (Eds.), *Infant education: A guide for helping handicapped children in the first three years.* New York: Walter.

Baroff, G.S. (Ed.). (1974). *Mental retardation: Nature, cause and management.* New York: Wiley.

Batshaw, M.L. & Perret, Y.M. (1981). *Children with handicaps: A medical primer.* Baltimore: Brookes.

*Baum, M.H. (1962). Some dynamic factors affecting family adjustment to the handicapped child. *Exceptional Children, 28,* 387-392.

Behrman, R.E. & Vaughan, V.C. III. (1983). *Nelson textbook of pediatrics* (12th ed.). Philadelphia: Saunders.

Belman, A.L., Novick, B., Ultmann, M.H., Spiro, A., Rubenstein, A., Horoupian, D.S., & Cohen, H. (1984). Neurologic complications in children with acquired immune deficiency syndrome (abstract). *Annals of Neurology, 16,* 414.

Benfield, G.D., Leib, S.A., & Reuter, J. (1976). Grief response of parents after referral of the critically ill newborn to a regional center. *New England Journal of Medicine, 294*(18), 975-978.

Berg, C. & Emanuel, I. (1983). Relationship of prenatal care to the prevention of mental retardation and other problems of pregnancy outcome. In E.M. Eklund (Ed.), *Developmental handicaps: Prevention and treatment II* (cooperative project between University Affiliated Facilities and State MCH/CC programs). Silver Spring, MD: American Association of University Affiliated Programs for Persons with Developmental Disabilities.

_____

(\*) Indicates additional references relevant to social work and mental retardation not cited elsewhere in this volume.

Berger, G.S., Gillings, D.B., & Siegel, E. (1976). The evaluation of regionalized perinatal health care programs. *American Journal of Obstetrics & Gynecology, 125,* 929-932.

*Bishop, K.K. (1984). Social work needs for genetics education. In J.K. Burns and C.A. Reiser (Eds.), *Genetic family history: An aid to better health in adoptive children.* Washington, DC: National Center for Education in Maternal and Child Health.

*Black, R.B. (1980). Support for genetic services: A survey. *Health & Social Work, 5,* 27-34.

*Black, R.B. (1981). Risk taking behavior: Decision making in the face of genetic uncertainty. *Social Work in Health Care, 7*(1), 11-25.

*Black, R.B. (1983). Genetics and adoption: A challenge for social work. In *Social work in a turbulent world.* Silver Spring, MD: National Association of Social Workers.

Blackman, J.A. (Ed.). (1983). *Medical aspects of developmental disabilities in children birth to three.* Iowa City: University of Iowa.

Bleck, E.E. & Nagel, D.A. (Eds.). (1975). *Physically handicapped children: A medical atlas for teachers.* New York: Grune & Stratton.

*Bracht, N.F. (1978). *Social work in health care: A guide to professional practice.* New York: Haworth Press.

*Brantley, D. (1980). A genetics primer for social workers. *Health & Social Work, 5,* 5-13.

*Brantley, M.D. & West S. (1983). The prevention of genetic disorders in underserved and rural areas. *Human Services in the Rural Environment, 8,* 3-8.

*Bregman, A.M. (1980). Living with progressive childhood illness: Parental management of neuromuscular disease. *Social Work in Health Care, 5*(4), 387-407.

Burney, L.R., Walker, A.P., & Dumars, K.W. (1984). Prenatal diagnosis: The state-of-the-art. In E.M. Eklund (Ed.), *Developmental handicaps: Prevention and treatment II* (cooperative project between University Affiliated Facilities and State MCH/CC programs). Silver Spring, MD: American Association of University Affiliated Programs for Persons with Developmental Disabilities.

Caldwell, M. (1982). Nutrition for the handicapped child. *Public Health Reports, 97,* 483-487.

Cassells, P. & Vermeersch, J. (1976). *Parents' guide to the galactose restricted diet.* Davis: California Department of Health, Maternal and Child Health Branch.

Child Abuse Prevention and Treatment Act of 1974 (Public Law 93-247), 42 U.S.C. 5101.

Chinn, P.C., Drew, C.J., & Logan, D.R. (1975). *Mental retardation: A life cycle approach.* St. Louis: Mosby.

*Cohen, P. (1962). The impact of the handicapped child on the family. *Social Casework, 43*(3), 137-142.

Crain, L.S. & Millor, G.K. (1978). Forgotten children: Maltreated children of mentally retarded parents. *Pediatrics, 61,* 130-132.

Crocker, A.C. (1982). Current strategies in prevention of mental retardation. *Pediatric Annals, 11*(5), 450-457.

Crowe, F.W., Schull, W.J. & Neel, J.V. (1952). *Multiple neurofibromatosis* (American Lecture Series No. 281). Springfield, IL: Charles C Thomas.

Cunningham, R.D. (1970). Endocrine diseases. In W.A. Daniel, Jr. (Ed.), *The adolescent patient.* St. Louis: Mosby.

*Cunningham, C.C. & Sloper, T. (1977). Parents of Down's syndrome babies: Their early needs. *Child Care, Health and Development, 3*(5), 325-347.

*Darling, R.B. (1977). Parents, physicians and spina bifida. *Hastings Center Report, 7*(4), 10-14.

Developmentally Disabled Assistance and Bill of Rights Act of 1984 (Public Law 98-527) 42 U.S.C.S. 6000 et seq.

Drillien, C. (1961). A longitudinal study of the growth and development of prematurely and maturely born children. *Archives of Diseases in Childhood 36*, 1-22.

Education for All Handicapped Children Act of 1975 (Public Law 94-142), 20 U.S.C. 1401 et seq.

Eklund, E.M. (Ed.). (1983). *Developmental handicaps: Prevention and treatment* (cooperative project between University Affiliated Facilities and State MCH/CC programs). Washington, DC: American Association of University Affiliated Programs for Persons with Developmental Disabilities.

Eklund, E.M. (Ed.). (1984). *Developmental handicaps: Prevention and treatment II* (cooperative project between University Affiliated Facilities and State MCH/CC programs). Silver Spring, MD: American Association of University Affiliated Programs for Persons with Developmental Disabilities.

Eklund, E.M. (Ed.). (1985). *Developmental handicaps: Prevention and treatment III* (cooperative project between University Affiliated Facilities and State MCH/CC programs). Silver Spring, MD: American Association of University Affiliated Programs for Persons with Developmental Disabilities.

*Evans, M.L. & Hansen, B.D. (1985). *A clinical guide to pediatric nursing* (2nd ed.). Norwalk, CT: Appleton-Century-Crofts.

*Fairfield, B. (1983). Parents coping with genetically handicapped children: Early recollections. *Exceptional Children, 49*(5), 411-414.

*Farber, B. (1968). *Mental retardation: Its social context and social consequences.* Boston: Houghton Mifflin.

*Federal research activity in mental retardation: A review with recommendations for the future.* (1977). Report of the Ad Hoc Consultants on Mental Retardation. Washington, DC: U.S. Government Printing Office.

*Finley, W.H. & Finley, S.A. (1970). Genetic disorders. In W.A. Daniel, Jr. (Ed.), *The adolescent patient.* St. Louis: Mosby.

*Fletcher, J.C. (1982). *Coping with genetic disorders: A guide for clergy and parents.* New York: Harper and Row.

Ford, F.R. (1966). *Diseases of the nervous system in infancy, childhood and adolescence,* (5th ed.). Springfield, IL: Charles C Thomas.

*Forsman, I. & Bishop, K.K. (Eds.). (1980). *Education in genetics: Nurses and social workers* (DHHS Pub. No. HSA 81-5120A). Washington, DC: U.S. Government Printing Office.

*Fost, N. (1981). Counseling families who have a child with a severe congenital anomaly. *Pediatrics, 67*(3), 321-324.

*Fowle, C.M. (1968). The effect of the severely mentally retarded child on his family. *American Journal of Mental Deficiency, 73*, 468-476.

Friedman, H.M. (1981). Cytomegalovirus: Subclinical infection or disease? *American Journal of Medicine, 70*, 215-217.

Gastel, B., Haddow, J.E., Fletcher, J.C. & Neale, A. (1980). *Maternal serum alpha-fetoprotein: Issues in the prenatal screening and diagnosis of neural tube defects.* Proceedings of a conference held by the U.S. Department of Health and Human Services, Public Health Service, Office of the Assistant Secretary for Health, Office of Health Research, Statistics and Technology; National Center for Health Care Technology; and the U.S. Food and Drug Administration.

Gayton, W.F. & Walker, L. (1974). Down syndrome: Informing the parents. *American Journal of Diseases of Children, 127,* 510-512.

Gellis, S.S., Feingold, M. & Rutman, J.Y. (1968). *Atlas of Mental retardation syndromes.* Washington, DC: U.S. Department of Health, Education, and Welfare, Social and Rehabilitation Service, Rehabilitation Services Administration Division of Mental Retardation.

*Goldstein, S.B. (1980). The effect of mainstreaming on self-esteem in adolescents and young adults with spina bifida. *Spina Bifida Therapy, 2*(4), 309-319.

Gordon, I (1969). *Early child stimulation through parent education: A final report to the Children's Bureau.* Gainesville: University of Florida Press.

Gorlin, R.J. (1981). Coffin-Lowry syndrome vs. Coffin-Siris syndrome: An example of confusion compounded. *American Journal of Medical Genetics, 10,* 103-104.

Gorlin, R.J., Pindborg, J.J., & Cohen, M. (1976). *Syndromes of the head and neck.* New York: McGraw-Hill.

Gramm-Rudman Federal Deficit Reduction Amendment of 1985, House Journal, Res. 372, *96th* Congress, Congress of the United States, 1985.

Gramm-Rudman is law. (1985, December). *Arc.GAO,* 1-2.

*Griffin, M.L., Kavanagh, M.S. & Sorenson, J.R. (1976). Genetic knowledge, client perspectives, and genetic counseling. *Social Work in Health Care, 2,* 171-180.

Grossman, H.J. (Ed.). (1983). *Classification in mental retardation.* Washington, DC: American Association on Mental Deficiencies.

*Haffner, D. (1980). *Learning together: A guide for families with genetic disorders.* (DHHS Pub. No. HSA 80-5131). Washington, DC: U.S. Government Printing Office.

Hagerman, R.J. (1984). Pediatric assessment of the learning-disabled child. *Developmental and Behavioral Pediatrics, 5,* 274-283.

Hagerman, R.J. & McBogg, P.M. (1983). *The fragile X syndrome.* Dillon, CO: Spectra.

Hagerman, R.J., McBogg, P., & Hagerman, P.J. (1983). The fragile X syndrome: History, diagnosis and treatment. *Developmental and Behavioral Pediatrics, 4,* 122-130.

Hall, B.D. & Smith, D.W. (1972). Prader-Willi syndrome. *Journal of Pediatrics, 81,* 286-293.

*Hall, W.T. & Young, C.L. (Eds.). (1977). *Genetic disorders: Social service interventions.* Proceedings of conference sponsored by Maternal and Child Health Services; and University of Pittsburgh, Graduate School of Public Health, Pittsburgh.

Hanshaw, J.B. (1964). Clinical significance of cytomegalovirus infections. *Postgraduate Medicine, 35,* 472-480.

Hanson, M. (1977). *Teaching your Down syndrome infant: A guide for parents.* Baltimore: University Park Press.

Harryman, S.E. (1976). Physical therapy. In R.B. Johnston & P.R. Magrab (Eds.), *Developmental disorders: Assessment, treatment, education.* Baltimore: University Park Press.

Harvey, J., Judge, C., & Wiener, S. (1977). Familial X-linked mental retardation with an X chromosome abnormality. *Journal of Medical Genetics, 14,* 46-50.

Haskins, R., Finkelstein, N., & Stedman, D. (1978). Infant stimulation programs and their effects. *Pediatric Annals, 7,* 123-143.

Haynes, U. (1980). *Risk factors. A developmental approach to case findings among infants and young children.* U.S. Department of Health & Human Services, Public Health Service, Health Services Administration, Bureau of Community Health Services, Office for Maternal and Child Health. Washington, DC: U.S. Government Printing Office.

Heber, R. (1971). *Rehabilitation of families at risk for mental retardation, A progress report.* Madison: University of Wisconsin Press.

*Henry, D.L., DeChristopher, J., Dowling, P., & Lapham, E.V. (1981). *Social Work in Education, 3,* 7-19.

*Hill, R. (1958). Generic features of families under stress. *Social Casework, 39,* 139-150.

Horejsi, C.R. (1979). Developmental disabilities: Opportunities for social workers. *Social Work, 24*(1), 40-43.

Howard-Peebles, P.N. & Finley, W.H. (1983). Screening of mentally retarded males for macro-orchidism and the fragile X chromosome. *American Journal of Medical Genetics, 15,* 631-635.

Hunter, A.G., Partington, M.W., & Evans, J.A. (1982). The Coffin-Lowry syndrome experience from four centres. *Clinical Genetics, 21,* 321-335.

*Illingsworth, R.S. (1967). Counseling the parents of the mentally handicapped child. *Clinical Pediatrics, 6,* 340-348.

Johnson, N.M. & Chamberlin, H.R. (1983). Early intervention: The state of the art. In E.M. Eklund (Ed.), *Developmental handicaps: Prevention and treatment* (cooperative project between University Affiliated Facilities and State MCH/CC programs). Silver Spring, MD: American Association of University Affiliated Programs for Persons with Developmental Disabilities.

Johnston, R.B. & Magrab, P.R. (Eds.). (1976). *Developmental disorders: Assessment, treatment, education.* Baltimore: University Park Press.

Kaminer, R.K. & Cohen, H.J. (1983). Intellectually limited mothers. In E.M. Eklund (Ed.), *Developmental handicaps: Prevention and treatment II* (cooperative project between University Affiliated Facilities and State MCH/CC programs). Silver Spring, MD: American Association of University Affiliated Programs for Persons with Developmental Disabilities.

*Kataria, S., Goldstein, D.J., & Kushnick, T. (1984). Developmental delays in Williams ("Elfin Facies") syndrome. *Applied Research in Mental Retardation, 5,* 419-423.

*Kirkman, H.N. (1978). Single-gene disorders. *Pediatric Annals, 7,* 54-70.

*Kirman, B. (1980). Growing up with Down's syndrome. *British Journal of Hospital Medicine, 23*(4), 385-388.

Koch, R., Azen, C., Friedman, E.G., & Williamson, M.L. (1984). Paired comparisons between early treated PKU children and their matched sibling controls on intelligence and school achievement test results at eight years of age. *Journal of Inherited Metabolic Diseases, 7,* 86-90.

*Kurtz, P.D. (1979). Early identification of handicapped children: A time for social work involvement. *Child Welfare, 58,* 165-176.

\*Kushner, H.S. (1983). *When bad things happen to good people.* New York: Avon Books.

\*Laurence, K.M. & Morris, J. (1981). The effect of the introduction of prenatal diagnosis on the reproductive history of women at increased risk from neural tube defects. *Prenatal Diagnosis, 1*(1), 51-60.

Lazar, I. & Darlington, R. (1982). *Lasting effects of early education: A report from the consortium for longitudinal studies* (Monographs of the Society for Research in Child Development).

Lemeshow, S. (1982). *The handbook of clinical types in mental retardation.* Boston: Allyn and Bacon.

Lenke, R.R. & Levy, H.L. (1980). Maternal phenylketonuria and hyperphenylalanemia: An international survey of the outcome of untreated and treated pregnancies. *New England Journal of Medicine, 303,* 1202-1208.

Levine, M.I. (1978). A pediatrician's view: A genetics primer. *Pediatric Annals, 7,* 7-12.

\*Levy, H.L. (1982). Maternal PKU: Control of an emerging problem. *American Journal of Public Health, 72*(12), 1320-1321.

Lieber, L.L. & Baker, J.M. (1976, September). *Parents anonymous: Self-help treatment for child abusing parents. A review and an evaluation.* Paper presented to the International Congress on Child Abuse and Neglect, Geneva, Switzerland.

Litch, S. (1978). *Towards the prevention of mental retardation in the next generation.* Ft. Wayne, IN: Fort Wayne Printing Co.

\*Lorincz, A.E. (1978). The mucopolysaccharidoses: Advances in understanding and treatment. *Pediatric Annals, 7,* 64-98.

Lubs, M.L.E. & Maes, J.A. (1977). Recurrence risk in mental retardation. In P. Mittler, (Ed.), *Research to practice in mental retardation: Vol. III. Biomedical aspects.* Baltimore: University Park Press.

\*Matheny, A. & Vernick, J. (1969). Parents of the mentally retarded child: Emotionally overwhelmed or informationally deprived? *Journal of Pediatrics, 74,* 953-959.

McGrath, F.C., O'Hara, D. & Thomas, D. (1978). *Instructional manual and evaluation guide: Graduate social work in the University-Affiliated Facility.* (DHEW Publication No. HSA 78-5226). U.S. Department of Health, Education and Welfare, Public Health Service, Health Services Administration, Bureau of Community Health Services. Washington, DC: U.S. Government Printing Office.

\*McKusick, V.A. (1983). *Mendelian inheritance in man* (6th ed). Baltimore: Johns Hopkins University Press.

Menkes, J.H. (1985). *Textbook of child neurology* (3rd ed.). Philadelphia: Lea & Febiger.

\*Mercer, R.T. (1974). Mothers' responses to their infants with birth defects. *Nursing Research, 23,* 133-137.

\*Milofsky, C. (1980). Serving the needs of disabled clients: A task-structured approach. *Social Work, 25,* 149-152.

Milunsky, A. (1975). *The prevention of genetic disease and mental retardation.* Philadelphia: W.B. Saunders.

\*Milunsky, A. (1977). *Know your genes.* New York: Avon Books.

\*Milunsky, A. & Annas, G.J. (Eds.). (1980). *Genetics and the law. II.* New York: Plenum Press.

*Murray, R.F. (1976). Psychological aspects of genetic counseling. *Social Work in Health Care, 2,* 13-24.

Myers, G.J., Cerone, S.B., & Olson, A.L. (Eds.). (1981). *A guide for helping the child with spina bifida.* Springfield, IL: Charles C Thomas.

National Housing Act, National Housing Act of 1976 (Public Law 94-375), 12 U.S.C.S. 1701.

Nyhan, W.L. (1981). Nutritional treatment of children with inborn errors of metabolism. In R.M. Suskind(Ed.), *Textbook of pediatric nutrition.* New York: Raven Press.

*Olshansky, S. (1962). Chronic sorrow: A response to having a mentally defective child. *Social Casework, 43*(4), 190-193.

*Omenn, G.S., Hall, J.G., & Hansen, K.D. (1980). Genetic counseling for adoptees at risk for specific inherited disorders. *American Journal of Medical Genetics, 5*(2), 157-164.

Omnibus Budget Reconciliation Act of 1981 (Public Law 97-35), 42 CFR Part 440. Authority: Sec. 1102 of the Social Security Act, 42 U.S.C. 1302, Federal Register, Vol. 50, No. 49, p. 10013.

Opitz, J.M. (1973). Klinefelter's syndrome. In D. Bergsma (Ed.), *Birth defects — Atlas and compendium.* Baltimore: Williams & Wilkins.

Palmer, S. & Ekvall, S. (1978). *Pediatric nutrition in developmental disorders.* Springfield, IL: Charles C Thomas.

*Parks, R.M. (1977). Parental reaction to the birth of a handicapped child. *Health and Social Work, 2,* 51-66.

Parmelee, A.H. & Haber, A. (1973). Who is the 'risk infant'? *Clinical Obstetrics & Gynecology, 16,* 376.

Piper, M. & Pless, I. (1980). Early intervention for infants with Down syndrome: A controlled trial. *Pediatrics, 65,* 463-467.

Pipes, P. (1978). Prader-Willi syndrome. In S. Palmer and S. Ekvall (Eds.), *Pediatric nutrition in developmental disorders.* Springfield, IL: Charles C Thomas.

*Plumridge, D. (1976). *Good things come in small packages: The whys and hows of Turner's syndrome.* Portland: University of Oregon Health Sciences Center.

*Plumridge, D., Barkost, C., & Lafranchi, S. (1982). *Klinefelter syndrome: The X-tra special boy.* Portland: University of Oregon Health Sciences Center.

President's Committee on Mental Retardation (1972). *Report of the Ad Hoc Consultant of Mental Retardation.* Washington, DC: U.S. Government Printing Office.

*Pueschel, S.M. & Yeatman, S. (1977). An educational and counseling program for phenylketonuric adolescent girls and their parents. *Social Work in Health Care, 3*(1), 29-36.

Rehabilitation Act of 1973 (Public Law 93-112), 29 U.S.C.S. 701 et seq.

Rehabilitation Amendments of 1984 (Public Law 98-221), 29 U.S.C.S. 701 et seq.

Report of the Surgeon General's workshop on breastfeeding and human lactation. (1984). U.S. Department of Health and Human Services, Public Health Service, Health Resources and Services Administration, Bureau of Health Care Delivery and Assistance, Division of Maternal and Child Health; in cooperation with the University of Rochester Medical Center, Rochester, NY.

*Riccardi, V. (1982). Early manifestatins of neurofibromatosis: Diagnosis and management. *Comprehensive Therapy, 8*(10), 35-40.

Richmond, J.B., Tarjan, G., & Mendelsohn, R.S. (1976). *Mental retardation: A handbook for the primary physician* (3rd ed.). Chicago: American Medical Association.

Rozovski, S.J. & Winick, M. (1979). Nutrition and cellular growth. In M. Winick (Ed.), *Human nutrition: A comprehensive treatise, I*. New York: Plenum Press.

Rubinstein, J.H. & Taybi, H. (1963). Broad thumbs and toes and facial abnormalities: A possible mental retardation syndrome. *American Journal of Diseases of Childhood, 105,* p. 588.

Rudolph, A.M. (Ed.). *Pediatrics* (17th ed.). Norwalk, CT: Appleton-Century-Crofts.

Runyan, D.K. & Gould, C.L. (1985). Foster care for maltreatment: II. Impact on school performance. *Pediatrics, 76*(5), 841-847.

*Salquero, C. (1980). A report on the Administration for Children and Youth and Families (ACYF) funded research and demonstration projects. *Children Today, 9*(6), 10-11.

Schild, S. (1964). Parents of children with phenylketonuria. *Children, 11,* 92-96.

*Schild, S. (1973). Social worker's contributions to genetic counseling. *Social Casework, 54,* 387-392.

*Schild, S. (1977). Social work with genetic problems. *Health and Social Work, 2,* 59-77.

*Schild, S. & Black, R.B. (1984). *Social work and genetics: A guide for practice.* New York: Haworth Press.

Schilling, R.F., Schinke, S.P., Blythe, B.J. & Barth, R.R. (1982). Child maltreatment and mentally retarded parents: Is there a relationship? *Mental Retardation, 20*(5), 201-209.

Schimke, R.N. (1978). Genetic disorders of sex differentiation. *Pediatric Annals, 7,* 39-51.

*Schultz, A.L. (1966). The impact of genetic disorders. *Social Work, 11*(2), 29-34.

Scrimshaw, N.S. (1969). Early malnutrition and central nervous system function. *Merrill-Palmer Quarterly, 15,* 375-387.

*Sensky, T. (1982). Family stigma in congenital physical handicap. *British Medical Journal, 285,* 1033-1035.

Smith, D.W. (1982). *Recognizable patterns of human malformation: Genetic, embryologic and clinical aspects* (3rd ed.). Philadelphia: Saunders.

Smith, M.A. (1978). Argininosuccinic aciduria. In S. Palmer & S. Ekvall (Eds.), *Pediatric nutrition in developmental disorders.* Springfield, IL: Charles C Thomas.

*Solnit, A. & Stark, M. (1961). Mourning and the birth of a defective child. *Psychoanalytic Study of the Child, 16,* 423-437.

Stagno, S., Pass, R.F., Meyer, E.D., Henderson, R.E., Moore, E.G., Walton, P.D., & Alford, C.A. (1982). Congenital cytomegalovirus infection: The relative importance of primary and recurrent maternal infection. *New England Journal of Medicine, 306,* 945-949.

Steele, S. (1985). *Nursing assessment of young children vulnerable to developmental delays.* Birmingham: University of Alabama at Birmingham, Chauncey Sparks Center for Developmental and Learning Disorders.

Summitt, R.L. (1978). Autosomal syndromes. *Pediatric Annals, 7,* 94-120.

Sutherland, G.R. & Ashforth, P.C. (1979). X-linked mental retardation with macroorchidism and the fragile site at Xq27 or 28. *Human Genetics, 48,* 117-120.

*The child with spina bifida (II): Psychological, educational and family concerns. (1982). *Clinical Proceedings: Children's Hospital National Medical Center, 38*(4), 189-236.

Thornton, J.B. (1983). Dentistry and the handicapped child. *Alabama Journal of Medical Sciences, 20*(1), 22-26.

*Venters, M. (1981). Familial coping with chronic and severe childhood illness: The case of cystic fibrosis. *Social Science and Medicine, 15A,* 289-297.

Vocational Education Amendments of 1975 (Public Law 94-482), 20 U.S.C.S. 2310.

Waisbren, S.E., Schnell, R.R., & Levy, H.L. (1980). Diet termination in children with phenylketonuria: A review of psychological assessments used to determine outcome. *Journal of Inherited Metabolic Diseases, 3,* 149-153.

*Walzer, S., Wolff, P.H., Bowen, D., Silbert A.R., Bashir, A.S., Gerald, P.S., & Richmond, J.B. (1977). A method for the longitudinal study of behavioral development in infants and children: The early development of XXY children. *Journal of Child Psychology and Psychiatry, 19*(3), 213-229.

*Weiss, J.O. (1976). Social work and genetic counseling. *Social Work in Health Care, 2-,* 5-12.

*Weiss, J.O. (1981). Psychosocial stress in genetic disorders: A guide for social workers. *Social Work in Health Care, 6,* 17-31.

Wenz, E. & Michell, M. (1978). Galactosemia. In S. Palmer and S. Ekvall (Eds.). *Pediatric nutrition in developmental disorders.* Springfield, IL: Charles C Thomas.

Williams, D.M. (1982). Coordinating comprehensive child health services. In D. Brantley & S. Wright (Eds.), *Coordinating comprehensive child health services: Service, training, and applied research perspectives.* Based on the proceedings of the 1981 Tri-Regional Workshop for Social Workers in Maternal and Child Health Services, sponsored by The University of Alabama at Birmingham, Chauncey Sparks Center for Developmental and Learning Disorders; and U.S. Department of Health and Human Services, Public Health Service, Health Services Administration, Bureau of Community Health Services, Office for Maternal and Child Health; Birmingham.

Wodarski, L.A. (1985). Nutrition intervention in developmental disabilities: An interdisciplinary approach. *Journal of the American Dietetic Association, 85,* 218-221.

Wolfensberger, W. (1967). Counseling parents of the retarded. In A. Baumeister (Ed.), *Appraisal, education, rehabilitation.* Chicago: Aldine.

Wolraich, M.L. (1983). Hydrocephalus. In J.A. Blackman (Ed.), *Medical aspects of developmental disabilities in children birth to three: A resource for special service providers in the educational setting.* Iowa City: University of Iowa.

*Wright, J.M. (1981). Fetal alcohol syndrome: The social work connection. *Health and Social Work, 6*(1), 5-10.

*Young, I.D. & Harper, P.S. (1981). Psychosocial problems in Hunter's syndrome. *Child Care, Health and Development, 7*(4), 201-209.

Ziai, M. (Ed.). (1984). *Pediatrics* (3rd ed.). Boston: Little, Brown.

# INDEX

case study, 119-121
characteristics, 118
diagnosis, 118
etiology, 118
incidence, 118
mental retardation, 118
signs and symptoms, 118
treatment concerns, 118-119
Williamson, M.L., 74, 145
Wilson disease, 73, 129
Winick, M., 34, 148
Wodarski, L.A., 35, 149
Wolfensberger, W., 22, 149
Wolff, P.H., 149
Wolraich, M.L., 123, 149
Wright, J.M., 149
Wright, S., 149

**X**

X-Linked definition, 139
X-Linked disorders, 91-92
X-Linked mental retardation
 Fragile X syndrome (*see* Fragile X syndrome)
 recognition of, 68

**Y**

Yeatman, S., 147
Young, C.L., 144
Young, I.D., 149

**Z**

Ziai, M., 106, 110, 149
Zygote, definition, 139